# TOUCHSTONE

## MICHAEL McCARTHY
## JEANNE McCARTEN
## HELEN SANDIFORD

# WORKBOOK

CAMBRIDGE
UNIVERSITY PRESS

CAMBRIDGE UNIVERSITY PRESS
Cambridge, New York, Melbourne, Madrid, Cape Town, Singapore, São Paulo, Delhi

Cambridge University Press
32 Avenue of the Americas, New York, NY 10013–2473, USA

www.cambridge.org
Information on this title: www.cambridge.org/9780521666107

First published 2005
9th printing 2009

Printed in Hong Kong, China, by Golden Cup Printing Company Limited

*A catalog record for this publication is available from the British Library*

ISBN  978-0-521-66611-4 pack consisting of student's book and self-study audio CD/CD-ROM (Windows®, Mac®)
ISBN  978-0-521-60129-0 pack consisting of student's book/Korea and self-study audio CD/CD-ROM (Windows®, Mac®)
ISBN  978-0-521-60130-6 pack consisting of student's book A and self-study audio CD/CD-ROM (Windows®, Mac®)
ISBN  978-0-521-60131-3 pack consisting of student's book B and self-study audio CD/CD-ROM (Windows®, Mac®)
ISBN  978-0-521-66610-7 workbook
ISBN  978-0-521-60132-0 workbook A
ISBN  978-0-521-60133-7 workbook B
ISBN  978-0-521-66609-1 teacher's edition
ISBN  978-0-521-66606-0 CDs (audio)
ISBN  978-0-521-66607-7 cassettes

*Art direction, book design, photo research, and layout services:* Adventure House, NYC
*Audio production:* Full House, NYC

# Contents

## Hello and good-bye

### Meetings and greetings

**Vocabulary** **A** Complete the conversations. Choose the correct response.

1. *A* Hello.
   *B* __Hi.__
   (a.) Hi.
   b. Good-bye.

2. *A* Hi. I'm Ted.
   *B* _____
   a. Hello, Ted. Nice to meet you.
   b. See you next week.

3. *A* How are you?
   *B* _____
   a. I'm Kyle.
   b. I'm fine, thanks.

4. *A* Good-bye.
   *B* _____
   a. See you later.
   b. Thanks.

5. *A* Good night.
   *B* _____
   a. Hello.
   b. Bye. See you tomorrow.

6. *A* Hi. How are you?
   *B* _____
   a. Good, thanks. How are you?
   b. Have a nice day.

**Vocabulary**

**B** Complete the conversations with the expressions in the box.

| Good night.   Have a good evening.   ✓Hello.   Hi.   How are you?   I'm fine   Nice to meet you.   See you |

1. *Jack* __Hello__ . I'm Jack.

    *Anna* _____ . I'm Anna.

    *Jack* _____ .

2. *Sonia* Hi, Julie. How are you?

    *Julie* Good. _____ ?

    *Sonia* _____ , thanks.

3. *Mike* _____ .

    *Koji* Thanks. You too.

4. *Joan* _____ .

    *Mary* Bye. _____ tomorrow.

**C** Complete the instant message.

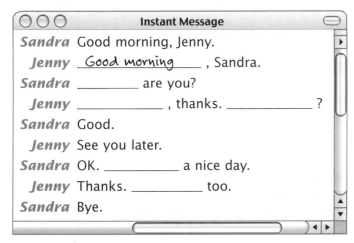

```
 ○○○              Instant Message

Sandra  Good morning, Jenny.
 Jenny  __Good morning__ , Sandra.
Sandra  _____ are you?
 Jenny  _____ , thanks. _____ ?
Sandra  Good.
 Jenny  See you later.
Sandra  OK. _____ a nice day.
 Jenny  Thanks. _____ too.
Sandra  Bye.
```

## 1 *My name's Michelle.*

| Vocabulary | Complete the conversation.

A  Good morning.

B  Good morning.

A  How are you?

B  I'm fine.

A  What's your __name__ ?

B  Michelle Browne.

A  How do you spell your _____ name ?

B  It's B-R-O-W-N-E.

A  And what's your _____ name?

B  Jean.

A  OK. How do you _____ *Jean*?

B  J-E-A-N.

A  And are you Ms., Miss, or _____ ?

B  Ms.

A  Thank you. Have a nice day.

B  Thanks. You too.

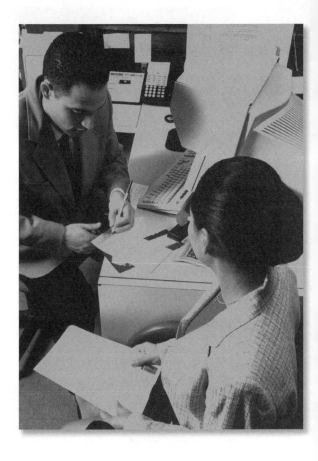

## 2 *Your personal information*

| Vocabulary | Complete the form. Use your own information.

### *Touchstone* English Classes

| | | |
|---|---|---|
| **Name:** | _____ | |
| | first          middle          last | |

☐ single      ☐ married

**Class:** _____

**Room:** _____

**Teacher:** _____

# 3 *Are we in the same class?*

**Grammar** **A** Complete the conversation. Write *am* or *are*. Use contractions *'m* or *'re* where possible.

*Receptionist* Hello. __Are__ you here for an
English class?

*Mi Young* Yes, I _____ . I'm Mi Young.

*Receptionist* Mi Young Lee? You_____ in Class C.

*Mi Young* Thank you.

*Sergio* Hi. _____ I in Class C, too? I'm Sergio.

*Receptionist* Yes, you _____ .

*Sergio* So we_____ in the same class.

*Receptionist* Wait. _____ you Sergio Rodrigues?

*Sergio* No, I_____ not. I'm Sergio Lopes.

*Receptionist* Oh, you_____ in Class D.
You_____ not in the same class.

**B** Complete the conversation.

*David* Hi. _____ _____ Julia Kim?

*Maria* No, _____ _____ . I'm Maria Martinez.

*David* Hi, Maria. I'm David. Nice to meet you.

*Maria* _____ _____ here for a dance class?

*David* Yes, _____ _____ . _____ _____ in
the same class?

*Maria* Yes, _____ _____ . We're in Class A.

*David* Oh, good.

# 4 *About you*

**Grammar** Answer the questions. Use your own information.

1. Are you in an English class?

   _____

2. Are you in a French class?

   _____

3. How are you today?

   _____

4. Are you and your friends in the same English class?

   _____

5. Are you married?

   _____

## 1 What's the number?

Vocabulary **A** Write the numbers.

| 0 | 1 | 2 | 3 | 4 | 5 |
|---|---|---|---|---|---|
| zero | _____ | _____ | _____ | _____ | _____ |

| 6 | 7 | 8 | 9 | 10 |
|---|---|---|---|---|
| _____ | _____ | _____ | _____ | _____ |

**B** Complete the crossword puzzle.

|   |   |   | 1. S | i | x |   |   | 2. |   |   |
|---|---|---|------|---|---|---|---|----|---|---|
|   |   |   |      |   |   | 3. |   |    |   |   |
|   |   | 4. |     |   |   |   |   |    |   |   |
| 5. |  |    |     |   |   |   |   |    |   |   |
|   |   |   | 6.   |   |   |   |   |    |   |   |
| 7. |  |    |     |   | 8. |   |   |    |   |   |

**Across**

1. two × three = ___six___
3. two + eight = _____
4. ten ÷ two = _____
5. six – four = _____
6. three + six = _____
7. five × zero = _____
8. six + two = _____

**Down**

1. ten – three = _____
2. eight – seven = _____
3. eight – five = _____
4. two × two = _____

## 2 What's the word?

Vocabulary The letters spell a word. Write each letter in the correct box below to see the word.

| 1. C | 3. H | 5. N | 7. E | 9. U |
|------|------|------|------|------|
| 2. O | 4. O | 6. T | 8. S | 10. T |

| ten | four | nine | one | three | eight | six | two | five | seven |
|-----|------|------|-----|-------|-------|-----|-----|------|-------|
|     |      |      | C   |       |       |     |     |      |       |

# 3 Here's your membership card.

**Grammar**  Look at Mark's student ID card. Write his answers in the conversation.

*Lee*  Hello. Are you a member of the club?

*Mark*  No, I'm not.

*Lee*  OK. Well, here's an application form.
So, what's your last name?

*Mark*  It's Brokaw    .  **or**  Brokaw    .
**or**  My last name's Brokaw    .

*Lee*  Thank you. And your first name?

*Mark*  _____ .

*Lee*  What's your middle initial, please?

*Mark*  _____ .

*Lee*  And what's your e-mail address?

*Mark*  _____ .

*Lee*  Your phone number?

*Mark*  _____ .

*Lee*  Are you an English student?

*Mark*  _____ .

*Lee*  What's your teacher's name?

*Mark*  _____ .

*Lee*  Thank you. Here's your membership card.
Have a nice day.

# 4 About you

**Grammar and vocabulary**  Write questions with *What's* and the words given. Then answer the questions with your own information.

1. *A*  What's your name _____ ?
         *(your name)*

   *B*  _____ .

2. *A*  _____ ?
         *(your telephone number)*

   *B*  _____ .

3. *A*  _____ ?
         *(your e-mail address)*

   *B*  _____ .

4. *A*  _____ ?
         *(your English teacher's name)*

   *B*  _____ .

# Are you here for the concert?

## *1 Good evening.*

**Conversation strategies**  Complete the conversations with the expressions in the box. Use each expression only one time.

| Good evening. | ✓ Hi | How about you? | How are you doing? | Thank you. | Yes |
|---|---|---|---|---|---|
| Pretty good. | Hello. | Nice to meet you. | Good-bye. | thanks | Yeah |

1. *Sam* Hi, Ali.

   *Ali* ___Hi___ , Sam. _____ ?

   *Sam* Good, thanks. How about you?

   *Ali* _____ .

   *Sam* Am I late?

   *Ali* _____ , you are, but it's OK.

   *Sam* Good. By the way, here's your book.

   *Ali* Oh, _____ .

2. *Joe* Good evening.

   *Clerk* _____ . What's your name, please?

   *Joe* Joe Johnson.

   *Clerk* Oh, yes. Mr. Johnson. Your room number is 10A. Here's your key.

   *Joe* _____ .

3. *Sally* Hello. My name's Sally.

   *Kate* _____ . I'm Kate. _____ .
   Are you here on business?

   *Sally* _____ , I am. _____ ?

   *Kate* No, I'm on vacation.

   *Sally* Nice. Oh, here's a taxi. _____ .

   *Kate* Bye.

# 2 *How are you doing?*

**A** Rewrite the conversation. Use less formal expressions for the underlined words.

A  <u>Hello. How are you?</u>

A  <u>Hi. How are you doing?</u>

B  <u>I'm fine, thank you.</u> How are you?

B  _____

A  I'm fine. Are you a student here?

A  _____

B  <u>Yes,</u> I am. How about you?

B  _____

A  <u>Yes,</u> me too.

A  _____

B  What's the e-mail address here?

A  It's Goodschool1@cup.org.

B  <u>Thank you. Good-bye.</u>

B  _____

A  <u>Good-bye.</u>

A  _____

**B** Number the lines of the conversation in the correct order. Then write the conversation.

____  Hi.

A  <u>Hello.</u> _____

____  Yeah, me too.

B  _____

____  OK.

A  _____

____  Are you here for the concert?

B  _____

____  How are you doing?

A  _____

_1_  Hello.

B  _____

____  Yeah, I am. How about you?

A  _____

## Unit 1 Progress chart

| Mark the boxes below to rate your progress. ✓ = I know how to . . .    ? = I need to review how to . . . | To review, go back to these pages in the Student's Book. |
|---|---|
| **Grammar** | |
| ☐ make statements with *I'm (not)*, *you're (not)*, and *we're (not)* | 2, 4, and 5 |
| ☐ ask questions with *Are you . . . ?* | 5 |
| ☐ ask questions with *What's . . . ?* | 4, 6, and 7 |
| ☐ give answers with *It's . . .* | 6 and 7 |
| **Vocabulary** | |
| ☐ say hello and good-bye in at least 4 different ways | 1, 2, and 3 |
| ☐ talk about names in English | 2 and 4 |
| ☐ say numbers 0–10 | 6 |
| **Conversation strategies** | |
| ☐ use *How about you?* | 8 |
| ☐ use everyday expressions in more formal and less formal situations | 9 |

# Unit 2 In class

Classmates

## 1 Where is everybody today?

Grammar | **A** Look at the pictures. Complete the sentences.

1. Bill __is__ at the gym. __He's__ not at home.

2. Jon and Karen _____ at home. _____ not in class.

3. Sun Yee _____ in the cafeteria. _____ late.

4. David _____ on vacation. _____ asleep.

5. Kate and Tess _____ in class. _____ not at the library.

6. Carmen _____ at work. _____ not sick.

**B** Complete the questions about the people in part A. Then answer the questions.

1. *A* __Is__ Bill at work?
   *B* __No, he's not._____

2. *A* _____ Jon and Karen at home?
   *B* _____

3. *A* _____ Sun Yee at the gym?
   *B* _____

4. *A* _____ David asleep?
   *B* _____

5. *A* _____ Kate and Tess on vacation?
   *B* _____

6. *A* _____ Carmen at work?
   *B* _____

## 2 Absent classmates

*Grammar*  **Complete the conversation with the verb *be*.
Use contractions where possible.
Add *not* where necessary.**

*Silvia*  Hi. How __are__ you?

*Jason*  Good, thanks. How about you?

*Silvia*  Pretty good. _____ Dave here?

*Jason*  No, he____ _____ .
I think he____ sick.

*Silvia*  Oh. _____ he at home?

*Jason*  I don't know.

*Silvia*  How about Jenny and Paula?
_____ they here?

*Jason*  No, they____ ____ . They____ on
vacation. I think they____ in Miami.

*Silvia*  Look! Dave____ not sick. He____ over
there. He____ just late again!

## 3 About you

*Grammar
and
vocabulary*  **Complete the questions with the names of your friends and classmates.
Then answer the questions.**

1. *A*  Is _Paul_____ at home?

   *B*  _Yes, he is._____

2. *A*  Are _____ and _____ at work?

   *B*  _____

3. *A*  Is _____ in class today?

   *B*  _____

4. *A*  Are _____ and _____ on vacation?

   *B*  _____

5. *A*  Are _____ and _____ in your English class?

   *B*  _____

6. *A*  Is _____ sick today?

   *B*  _____

7. *A*  Is _____ at the library?

   *B*  _____

8. *A*  Are _____ and _____ asleep?

   *B*  _____

# What's in your bag?

## 1 Everyday things

*Vocabulary* Label the things in the picture.

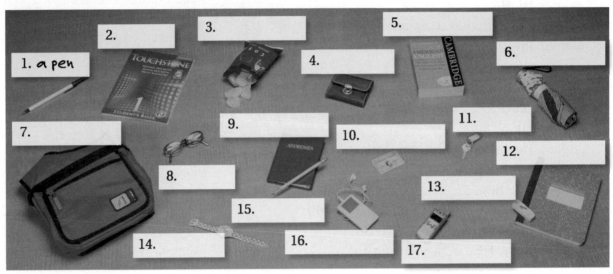

1. a pen
2.
3.
4.
5.
6.
7.
8.
9.
10.
11.
12.
13.
14.
15.
16.
17.

## 2 What are these things?

*Grammar and vocabulary* Write sentences about the pictures.

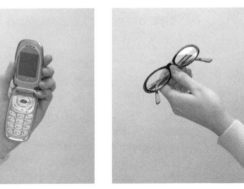

1.  This is a bag.    2.  These are pens.    3. _____    4. _____

5. _____    6. _____    7. _____    8. _____

# *3* **Asking about things**

**Grammar** **Complete the conversations. Use the words in the box.**

| Is | it | it's | these | they're | this | What |
|---|---|---|---|---|---|---|
| Is | it | these | they | they're | this | ✓What's |

1. **Clerk** You're in Room 102.
   **Ms. Simms** Thanks. __What's__ this?
   **Clerk** Oh, _____ your room key.
   **Ms. Simms** OK. Thank you.
   **Clerk** And _____ is your membership card for the fitness club.

2. **Erica** What's _____ ? _____ it a cell phone?
   **Jim** Yes, _____ is. It's a cell phone and an MP3 player.
   **Erica** I see.
   **Jim** _____ are these?
   **Erica** I think _____ watches.

3. **Bob** What are _____ ?
   **Jill** Oh, no! I think _____ my jeans.
   **Bob** Oh, I'm sorry. Are _____ new?
   **Jill** Yeah. Oh, look. _____ this your wallet?
   **Bob** Yes, _____ is.
   **Jill** Oh, no! And _____ are your credit cards!

## 1 Classroom things

Vocabulary    **A** Write the words under the pictures.

1. ___a board___    2. ___some posters___    3. _____    4. _____

5. _____    6. _____    7. _____    8. _____

9. _____    10. _____    11. _____    12. _____

**B** Circle the words from part A in the puzzle. Look in these directions (→↓).

| T | V | C | Q | U | A | B | L | A | M | A | B |
|---|---|---|---|---|---|---|---|---|---|---|---|
| W | E | H | A | S | I | C | U | Y | A | Z | O |
| A | C | A | L | E | N | D | A | R | P | H | A |
| G | O | I | H | K | O | P | Z | O | E | O | R |
| I | P | R | P | E | D | L | F | L | T | E | D |
| W | A | S | T | E | B | A | S | K | E | T | I |
| R | K | T | O | R | R | Y | O | O | M | U | M |
| O | C | U | O | S | J | E | C | D | E | S | K |
| N | L | L | G | T | O | R | X | I | T | J | A |
| C | O | M | P | U | T | E | R | O | T | D | S |
| M | C | A | S | M | P | O | S | T | E | R | S |
| A | K | I | V | I | D | E | O | S | V | A | R |

## 2 A classroom

**A** Look at the picture. Complete the sentences. Use the words in the box

| in | in | in front of | next to | ✓on | on | on | under |

1. The dictionaries are _____on_____ the floor.
2. The students' papers are _____ the wall.
3. The CD player is _____ the teacher's desk.
4. The calendar is _____ the wastebasket.
5. The videos are _____ the closet.
6. The computer is _____ the teacher's desk.
7. The teacher's desk is _____ the board.
8. The closet is _____ the window.

**B** Write the questions about the classroom in part A.

1. *A* _Where's the teacher's desk?_____

   *B* It's in front of the board.

2. *A* _____

   *B* It's next to the window.

3. *A* _____

   *B* They're on the floor.

4. *A* _____

   *B* It's under the teacher's desk.

5. *A* _____

   *B* They're on the wall.

6. *A* _____

   *B* It's in the wastebasket.

## 3 Missing apostrophes

Put apostrophes (') in the correct places in the questions. Then answer the questions.

1. What's your English teacher's name?     _____

2. What are your friends names?     _____

3. Whats on the wall in your classroom?     _____

4. Wheres your teacher now?     _____

# What's the word for this in English?

## 1 Questions, questions

*Conversation strategies*

**Complete the conversations. Use the expressions in the box.**

| ✓Excuse me | Thanks anyway. | Sure. | Here you go. | Thanks. |
|---|---|---|---|---|
| Can I borrow | You're welcome. | please | How do you spell | Sorry. |
| What's the word for this in English? | | | | |

1. *Callie* __Excuse me__ , Bob.
   *Bob* Yeah?
   *Callie* _____ your dictionary?
   *Bob* Sure. Now, where is it?
   *Callie* Um . . . it's right in front of you.
   *Bob* Oh, yeah. _____ .
   *Callie* Thanks.
   *Bob* _____ .

2. *Ruby* Can I borrow your cell phone, _____ ?
   *Millie* _____ . Oh, wait. It's not in my bag. I think it's at home. _____ .
   *Ruby* That's OK. _____ .
   *Millie* Sure. . . . _____ ?
   *Ruby* In English, the word is *umbrella*.
   *Millie* Umbrella? Thanks.
   *Ruby* Sure.

3. *Yuri* _____ *videos*?
   *Dan* V-I-D-E-O-S.
   *Yuri* _____ .
   *Dan* Sure.
   *Yuri* And how do you spell *television*?
   *Dan* T-V.
   *Yuri* Very funny!

# *2 Scrambled conversations*

Conversation strategies **Number the lines of the conversations in the correct order. Then write the conversations.**

1. _____ I'm sorry.                          A   You're late. _____
   __1__ You're late.                         B   _____
   _____ That's OK.                           A   _____

2. _____ Sure.                               A   _____
   _____ Thank you.                          B   _____
   _____ Can I borrow your pen, please?      A   _____
   _____ You're welcome.                     B   _____

3. _____ I don't know.                       A   _____
   _____ That's OK. Thanks anyway.           B   _____
   _____ That's OK. What about this?         A   _____
   _____ I'm sorry. I don't know.            B   _____
   _____ What's the word for this?           A   _____

# *Unit 2 Progress chart*

| **Mark the boxes below to rate your progress.**<br>☑ = I know how to . . .   ? = I need to review how to . . . | To review, go back to these pages in the Student's Book. |
|---|---|
| **Grammar** | |
| ☐ make statements with *he's (not)*, *she's (not)*, and *they're (not)* | 12 and 13 |
| ☐ ask questions with *Is he . . . ?*, *Is she . . . ?*, and *Are they . . . ?* | 13 |
| ☐ use *a* or *an* | 14 |
| ☐ make nouns plural with *-s*, *-es*, or *-ies* | 15 |
| ☐ use *this* with singular nouns and *these* with plural nouns | 14 and 15 |
| ☐ ask questions with *Where . . . ?* | 17 |
| ☐ use *'s* and *s'* to show possession | 17 |
| **Vocabulary** | |
| ☐ name at least 8 things students take to class | 14 and 15 |
| ☐ name at least 12 classroom items | 16 and 17 |
| ☐ say where things are in the classroom | 16 and 17 |
| **Conversation strategies** | |
| ☐ ask for help in class | 18 |
| ☐ use common responses to *Thank you* and *I'm sorry* | 19 |

## Celebrities

### 1 Favorites

Vocabulary   **A** Unscramble the letters. Write the words.

1. rgiens  singer

2. ctrao  a_____

3. rtweir  w_____

4. maet  t_____

5. ralype  p_____

6. dnab  b_____

7. hwso  s_____

8. prsot  s_____

9. naf  f_____

10. ivome  m_____

11. rtiats  a_____

**B** Complete the crossword puzzle with the words in part A.

**Across**

2. What's your favorite TV _show_ ?

4. Norah Jones is an amazing _____ .

6. Our favorite soccer _____ is Manchester United.

9. Meryl Streep is a great _____ .

11. Ronaldo is a famous soccer _____ .

**Down**

1. Soccer is a _____ .

3. Stephen King is a famous _____ .

5. Who's your favorite _____ ?

7. This _____ is exciting.

8. My favorite _____ is the Black Crowes.

10. Brian is a _____ of the Williams sisters.

## 2 *She's my favorite singer.*

**Grammar** Look at the pictures, and complete the sentences.

1. " She's my favorite singer. Her new CD is great."

2. "_____ Jama fans. Jama is _____ favorite band."

3. "_____ a great writer. _____ new book is really good."

4. "_____ favorite TV show is *The Visitors*. What's _____ favorite show?"

5. "_____ my favorite actors. I think _____ movies are very good."

6. "Cassandra Coe is my teacher. _____ a great artist. _____ pictures are amazing."

## 3 *They're great!*

**Grammar** Complete the conversation with the verb *be*. Use contractions where possible.

*Alicia* Look! It's Enrique Iglesias's new CD. He's____ my favorite singer.

*Norah* Yeah. I____ a big fan of his, too. His voice _____ amazing. Oh. Here's my favorite band.

*Alicia* Yeah? What's your favorite band?

*Norah* The Backstreet Boys. They____ great.

*Alicia* Yes, they _____ . Nick Carter _____ really good-looking. He____ my favorite.

# People we know

## 1 What are they like?

**Vocabulary** Look at the pictures, and complete the sentences. Use the words in the box.

| | | | | | |
|---|---|---|---|---|---|
| busy | fun | lazy | ✓quiet | smart | tired |
| friendly | interesting | outgoing | shy | strict | |

1. She's ____quiet____ and _____ .

2. He's _____ .

3. They're _____ .

4. She's _____ .

5. She's _____ .

6. He's _____ .

7. He's not very _____ or _____ .

8. They're _____ . She's _____ .

## 2 *What's new?*

Grammar   **Complete the conversation with the verb *be*. Use contractions where possible.
Add *not* where necessary.**

*Carrie*   Sorry. __Am__ I late?

*Josh*   No, you____ _____ . You____ fine.

*Carrie*   Good. So, what's new? _____ you busy at work?

*Josh*   Yes, I _____ . Our boss _____ sick, so
he____ _____ at work.

*Carrie*   Oh, really?

*Josh*   So how about you? What _____ your new
neighbors like? _____ they nice?

*Carrie*   Yes, they _____ . They____ OK. They____
very quiet.

*Josh*   _____ they students?

*Carrie*   No, they____ _____ . The guy _____ a writer.

*Josh*   A writer? What about the woman? _____ she a
writer, too?

*Carrie*   No, she____ _____ . She____ _____ a writer –
she____ a teacher. At our school!

## 3 *I'm not, you're not*

Grammar   **Rewrite the sentences in the negative form.**

1.  My neighbors are very nice.     My neighbors aren't very nice.

2.  My best friend is a student.    _____

3.  I'm very shy.    _____

4.  The students in my class are very smart.    _____

5.  My English class is easy.    _____

6.  My teacher is very quiet.    _____

## 4 *About you*

Grammar
and
vocabulary

**Complete the questions. Then write short answers. Add more information.**

1.  __Are__ you outgoing?     Yes, I am. I'm very outgoing.
    **or**   No, I'm not. I'm not outgoing.

2.  ____ your best friend lazy?    _____

3.  ____ your English class hard?    _____

4.  ____ your friends smart?    _____

5.  ____ your teacher fun?    _____

6.  ____ your classmates nice?    _____

7.  ____ you tired today?    _____

8.  ____ you and your friends busy after class?    _____

**21**

## 1 Who's who?

Vocabulary   Use the family tree to complete the sentences about this family.

1. David is Paul's
   <u>s  o  n</u> .

2. John is Katy's
   ___ ___ ___ ___ ___ ___ .

3. Katy is Paul's
   ___ ___ ___ ___ .

4. Josh, David, and Emily are Paul and Katy's
   ___ ___ ___ ___ ___ ___ ___ ___ .

5. Emily is Josh's
   ___ ___ ___ ___ ___ ___ ___ .

6. Josh is David's
   ___ ___ ___ ___ ___ ___ ___ .

7. John and Catherine are Katy's
   ___ ___ ___ ___ ___ ___ ___ ___ .

8. Katy is Josh's
   ___ ___ ___ ___ ___ .

9. John is Catherine's
   ___ ___ ___ ___ ___ ___ ___ .

10. Emily is Katy's
    ___ ___ ___ ___ ___ ___ ___ ___ .

11. Catherine is David's
    ___ ___ ___ ___ ___ ___ ___ ___ ___ ___ ___ .

12. John is Emily's
    ___ ___ ___ ___ ___ ___ ___ ___ ___ ___ ___ .

## 2 What's the number?

Vocabulary   Write the numbers.

1. ___sixty-five___   2. _____   3. _____   4. _____

5. _____   6. _____   7. _____   8. _____

## 3 *How about your children?*

**Unscramble the questions. Then write the answers to complete the conversations.**

1. are / your / How / children ?

    *A* <u>How are your children?</u>

    *B* They're fine, thanks. How about your children?

    *A* <u>They're OK.</u>

2. your / What / are / names / parents' ?

    *A* _____

    *B* George and Laura. How about your parents?

    *A* _____

3. is / grandfather / How / your / old ?

    *A* _____

    *B* He's 74. And your grandfather?

    *A* _____

4. mother / What's / your / like ?

    *A* _____

    *B* My mother? She's great. She's very smart. How about your mother?

    *A* _____

5. from / father / Where's / your ?

    *A* _____

    *B* Texas. How about your father?

    *A* _____

6. old / your / is / How / best friend ?

    *A* _____

    *B* She's 16. How about your best friend?

    *A* _____

## 4 *A famous family*

**Read part of a phone interview with an actor. Then write questions for the answers.**

*Interviewer* Hello, Kate. How are you?

   *Kate* Hi. I'm fine, thanks.

*Interviewer* Kate, I love your movies.

   *Kate* Thank you.

*Interviewer* Now, about your family . . . who's your mother?

   *Kate* Gwen Russell – the artist. And Kevin Russell is my father.

*Interviewer* Yes, they're famous! What are your parents like at home?

   *Kate* Oh, Dad's fun and outgoing. And Mom's very smart!

*Interviewer* And, Kate, what's your favorite band?

   *Kate* Green Day. They're amazing. . . .

1. <u>How is Kate?</u>

    She's fine.

2. _____

    Her mother is Gwen Russell.

3. _____

    Her father is fun and outgoing. Her mother is very smart.

4. _____

    Her favorite band is Green Day.

# *This is a friend of mine.*

## *1 New neighbors and co-workers*

**Conversation strategies**

**Complete the conversations with the questions in the box.**

| | | | |
|---|---|---|---|
| How old is she? | Where is she from? | ✓What are they like? | An actor? Is she good? |
| From Chile? | Are they friendly? | Are they good? | Where are they from? |

1. *Ming* Who are they?

   *Jim* Oh, they're my new neighbors.

   *Ming* Your neighbors? <u>What are they like</u> ?

   *Jim* Interesting. Very interesting. They're in a rock band.

   *Ming* A rock band? _____ ?

   *Jim* They're from New York.

   *Ming* Wow! _____ ?

   *Jim* No, they're not.

   *Ming* Uh-oh. _____ ?

   *Jim* Oh, very. Their friends are always here!

2. *Carlos* Who's she?

   *Kim* Her name's Angie.

   *Carlos* Angie? _____ ?

   *Kim* I don't know exactly. I think she's from Chile.

   *Carlos* _____ ? Really? What's she like?

   *Kim* She's outgoing and fun.

   *Carlos* Really? _____ ?

   *Kim* I'm not sure. Maybe 24 or 25.

   *Carlos* Oh. What's her job? Is she a server here?

   *Kim* Well, yes. But she's an actor, too.

   *Carlos* _____ ?

   *Kim* Yeah, she's a good actor but not a great server.

# 2 *Really? I'm surprised!*

**Conversation strategies**

Write responses to show you are interested or surprised. Then ask a question.

1. My grandmother's name is Banu.  | Really? What's she like? ___
2. My brother is a singer in a band. | ___
3. My grandfather is a tennis player. | ___
4. I'm from Alaska. | ___
5. My mother is a Spanish teacher. | ___
6. My new job is hard work. | ___
7. My sister is an artist. | ___
8. My last name is Oh. | ___

## Unit 3 Progress chart

| Mark the boxes below to rate your progress. ☑ = I know how to . . .    ? = I need to review how to . . . | To review, go back to these pages in the Student's Book. |
|---|---|
| **Grammar** | |
| ☐ use *my*, *your*, *his*, *her*, *our*, and *their* | 22 and 23 |
| ☐ make statements with *be* | 22 and 23 |
| ☐ ask *yes-no* questions with *be* | 24 and 25 |
| ☐ make negative statements with *be* | 24 and 25 |
| ☐ ask information questions with *be* | 26 and 27 |
| **Vocabulary** | |
| ☐ name at least 8 words to describe people's personalities | 24 and 25 |
| ☐ name at least 12 family words | 26 and 27 |
| ☐ say numbers 10–101 | 26 |
| **Conversation strategies** | |
| ☐ show interest by repeating information and asking questions | 28 |
| ☐ use *Really?* to show interest or surprise | 29 |

# Unit 4 Everyday life

**In the morning**

## 1 What's Kathy's morning like?

**Grammar and vocabulary**

**A** Complete the sentences about Kathy's morning. Use the correct form of the verbs in the box.

| check | exercise | get up | play |
|-------|----------|--------|------|
| eat   | ✓ get up | listen | read |

1. Kathy _gets up_ early. Her son _____ late.

2. She _____ before work. Her son _____ games.

3. She _____ to the radio in the car.

4. She and her co-workers _____ breakfast together.

5. Kathy _____ her e-mail right after breakfast.

6. Her boss _____ the newspaper at work.

**B** Rewrite the sentences in the negative form.

1. Kathy's son gets up early. _Kathy's son doesn't get up early._

2. Kathy checks her e-mail before breakfast. _____

3. Kathy and her son talk a lot in the morning. _____

4. Kathy's son does his homework. _____

5. Kathy and her boss eat breakfast together. _____

6. Kathy's boss plays computer games. _____

## 2 Guess what!

**Grammar**   Complete Peter's e-mail with the correct form of the verbs.

---

○○○                                    e-mail

Hi!
Guess what! I ___have___ (have) a new job – in a coffee shop. It's hard work.
I _____ (get up) early, and I _____ (work) late. But the coffee is good.

My boss is nice. He's French, and he _____
(study) English at night. He _____ (do) his
homework in the coffee shop. I _____ (help)
him sometimes. He's quiet, and he _____
(not / talk) a lot. He _____ (listen) to the radio
and _____ (sing), but we _____ (not / like)
the same music. He _____ (like) coffee, too. We
both _____ (have) four cups of coffee every day!

Write soon!
Peter

---

## 3 Typical morning activities

**Grammar and vocabulary**   **A**  What are typical morning activities? Match the verbs with the words and expressions.

| | |
|---|---|
| 1. do ___d___ | a. to the radio |
| 2. study _____ | b. (my) e-mail or messages |
| 3. check _____ | c. a car |
| 4. listen _____ | d. (my) homework |
| 5. drive _____ | e. an alarm clock |
| 6. play _____ | f. English |
| 7. read _____ | g. games on the computer |
| 8. use _____ | h. a book |

**B**  Write true sentences about your morning routine. Use the verbs in part A.

1. _I don't do my homework in the morning._
2. _____
3. _____
4. _____
5. _____
6. _____
7. _____
8. _____

## 1 *What's fun? What's not?*

**Vocabulary** **A** Which routine activities are fun for you? Complete the charts. Add your own ideas.

| | | | |
|---|---|---|---|
| check e-mail | do the laundry | get up early | ✓play sports |
| clean the house | drive to work | go shopping | take lessons / a class |
| do homework | eat snacks | make phone calls | watch TV |

| Fun! | |
|---|---|
| play sports | |
| | |
| | |
| | |

| Not fun! | |
|---|---|
| | |
| | |
| | |
| | |

**B** Write the days of the week in the date book. Then write one thing you do each day.

**S**unday: I go shopping on Sundays.
M_____: _____
T_____: _____
W_____: _____

Th_____: _____
F_____: _____
S_____: _____

## 2 *About you 1*

**Grammar and vocabulary** Use time expressions to write one thing you do and one thing you don't do.

1. on the weekends   I clean the house on the weekends.
   I don't go to work on the weekends.

2. after work / school   _____
   _____

3. every day   _____
   _____

4. on Saturdays   _____
   _____

5. in the afternoons   _____
   _____

6. at night   _____
   _____

## 3 What's your week like?

**Grammar** Complete the conversation with the correct form of the verbs.

*Cecilia* What's your week like, Eduardo? __Do__
(Do / Does)

you __go__ to work every day?
(go / goes)

*Eduardo* Well, no, I _____ . I work at home on Fridays.
(don't /doesn't)

*Cecilia* Really? What about the weekends? _____
(Do / Does)

you _____ then, too?
(work / works)

*Eduardo* Yes, I _____ . But I don't like it. What
(do / does)

about you? _____ you and your husband
(Do / Does)

_____ to work every day?
(go / goes)

*Cecilia* Yes, we _____ . But just Monday to Friday.
(do / does)

We _____ the house on the weekends.
(clean / cleans)

Oh, and we _____ to soccer games.
( go / goes)

*Eduardo* Oh. _____ your son _____ soccer?
(Do / Does)        (play / plays)

*Cecilia* Yes, he _____ . He's on the school team.
(do / does)

_____ your son _____ any sports?
(Do / Does)        (play / plays)

*Eduardo* No, he _____ . He plays games on the computer.
(don't / doesn't)

## 4 About you 2

**Grammar and vocabulary** Complete the questions. Then write answers with your own information.

1. *A* __Do__ you __take__ a class at night?

   *B* __Yes, I do. I take a Spanish class on Monday evenings.__

2. *A* _____ your father _____ TV before bed?

   *B* _____

3. *A* _____ you and your friends _____ shopping on Saturdays?

   *B* _____

4. *A* _____ your friends _____ their e-mail before breakfast?

   *B* _____

5. *A* _____ your mother _____ the newspaper every day?

   *B* _____

## 1 *Saying more than* yes *or* no

Conversation strategies

**A** Complete the conversation. Use the sentences in the box.

| |
|---|
| I work part-time in the cafeteria.      It's fun, and the people are nice. |
| Just Mondays and Wednesdays.        I'm an English student. |
| ✓ I'm new here, and I'm late.          I go there Mondays after work. It's great! |

*Mike*  Hi. Are you OK? You look lost.

*Yumi*  Hello. Where's Room 106? Do you know?

        I'm new here, and I'm late.

*Mike*  Yeah. It's right over there, next to the cafeteria.

*Yumi*  Thanks. So, do you work here?

*Mike*  Yes, I do. _____

*Yumi*  Do you like it? I mean, do you like the job?

*Mike*  Yeah, I do. _____

*Yumi*  That's good. Do you work here every day?

*Mike*  Well, no. _____

        I go to class on Tuesdays and Thursdays.

*Yumi*  Oh. So you're a student, too?

*Mike*  Yeah. _____

*Yumi*  Really? I'm an English student, too. Do you belong
to the English Club?

*Mike*  Yes, I do. _____

*Yumi*  Oh. Well, thanks a lot. And see you at English Club!

*Mike*  Great!

**B** Read the completed conversation again. Then read the sentences below.
Are they true or false? Check (✓) true or false.

| | True | False |
|---|:---:|:---:|
| 1. Mike and Yumi are friends. | ☐ | ✓ |
| 2. Mike works in the cafeteria. | ☐ | ☐ |
| 3. Mike is a new student. | ☐ | ☐ |
| 4. Mike works Tuesdays and Thursdays. | ☐ | ☐ |
| 5. Mike likes his part-time job. | ☐ | ☐ |
| 6. Yumi and Mike are English students. | ☐ | ☐ |
| 7. Mike belongs to the English Club. | ☐ | ☐ |

## 2 About you

**Unscramble the questions. Then answer the questions. Write more than**
*yes* **or** *no.* **Use** *Well* **if you need to.**

1. live / you / around / Do / here ?

   Do you live around here?

2. from / originally / you / here / Are ?

3. a / full-time / you / Are / student ?

4. have / you / brothers / Do / sisters / or ?

5. you / work / the / on / weekends / Do ?

6. Do / English / like / you / class / your ?

7. get up / day / you / Do / every / early ?

8. grandparents / Do / with / your / live / you ?

## 1 *Watching TV*

**Reading**  **A** **What do you think? What do average Americans do after work and school? Check (✓) the boxes.**

| | | |
|---|---|---|
| ☐ spend time with family | ☐ read | ☐ watch TV |
| ☐ go out with friends | ☐ go out to dinner | ☐ go shopping |

**B** **Read the article. Check your answers in part A.**

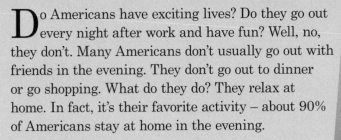

# After Work and School

Do Americans have exciting lives? Do they go out every night after work and have fun? Well, no, they don't. Many Americans don't usually go out with friends in the evening. They don't go out to dinner or go shopping. What do they do? They relax at home. In fact, it's their favorite activity – about 90% of Americans stay at home in the evening.

And what about young people? Well, they spend a lot of time at home, too. American high school students study for 3 hours a week and watch TV for 18 hours a week.

So, are Americans lazy? No, they're not. 80% of Americans have hobbies. Hobbies are fun, interesting, free-time activities – like sports, reading, music, and computers. Americans stay busy!

**Here are the average American's favorite activities in the evening:**

**26%** watch TV or videos

**25%** spend time with their families

**9%** read

**8%** go out with friends

**5%** go out to dinner

**C** **Read the article again. Then correct these false sentences.**

1. Americans go out every night after work.
   <u>Americans don't usually go out with friends in the evening.</u>

2. After work, Americans usually go shopping.
   _____

3. American high school students usually study for three hours a night.
   _____

4. American high school students don't watch TV.
   _____

5. 20% of Americans have hobbies.
   _____

## 2 *TV shows*

Writing **A** Read the e-mail messages. Then rewrite Joe's message. Use capital letters and **periods.**

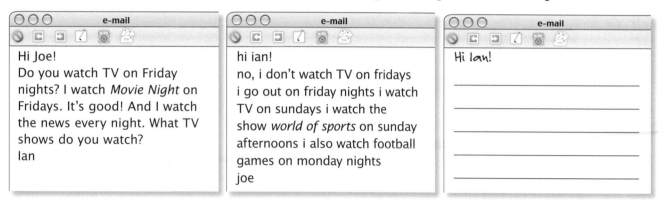

**Hi Joe!**
Do you watch TV on Friday nights? I watch *Movie Night* on Fridays. It's good! And I watch the news every night. What TV shows do you watch?
Ian

**hi ian!**
no, i don't watch TV on fridays i go out on friday nights i watch TV on sundays i watch the show *world of sports* on sunday afternoons i also watch football games on monday nights
joe

**Hi Ian!**
_____
_____
_____
_____
_____

**B** What TV shows do you watch? When do you watch them? Write an e-mail to a friend about your TV-watching habits.

Hi _____ !
_____
_____
_____
_____
_____
_____
_____

## Unit 4 Progress chart

| Mark the boxes below to rate your progress.<br>☑ = I know how to . . .     ? = I need to review how to . . . | To review, go back to these pages in the Student's Book. |
|---|---|
| **Grammar** ☐ make simple present statements | 34 and 35 |
| ☐ ask simple present *yes-no* questions and give short answers | 36 and 37 |
| **Vocabulary** ☐ name at least 12 new verbs for routine activities | 34, 35, 36, and 37 |
| ☐ name the days of the week | 36 |
| ☐ name at least 8 time expressions with the simple present | 37 |
| **Conversation strategies** ☐ answer questions with more than *yes* or *no* | 38 and 39 |
| ☐ use *Well* to get time to think of an answer | 39 |
| **Writing** ☐ use capital letters and periods | 41 |

# Unit 5 Free time

Going out

## 1 In your free time

*Vocabulary* How often do you do these things? Complete the chart with the free-time activities in the box. Add your own ideas.

| ✓ eat out | go out with friends | go to a club | go to a movie | play a sport |
|---|---|---|---|---|
| go on the Internet | go shopping | go to the gym | have dinner with family | rent a movie |

| *every day* | *three or four times a week* | *once or twice a week* | *once or twice a month* |
|---|---|---|---|
| | | eat out | |
| | | | |
| | | | |
| | | | |

## 2 Craig's busy schedule

*Grammar and vocabulary*

**A** Read Craig's calendar. Are the sentences below true or false? Write *T* (true) or *F* (false). Then correct the false sentences.

| *Sunday* | *Monday* | *Tuesday* | *Wednesday* | *Thursday* | *Friday* | *Saturday* |
|---|---|---|---|---|---|---|
| 5 | 6 | 7 | 8 | 9 | 10 | 11 |
| *morning:* do the laundry!! | *morning:* classes | *morning:* go to the gym!! | *morning:* classes | *morning:* go to the gym!! | *morning:* classes | *morning:* clean the house!! |
| | *afternoon:* go shopping | *afternoon:* library | *afternoon:* guitar lesson | | | *afternoon:* tennis with Bob |
| *evening:* dinner with Mom and Dad | | | | *evening:* dinner with Sandra | *evening:* movie with Jim | *evening:* club with Bill |

**Weekly Planner**

1. He goes out with friends ~~every night~~. _F_  *three nights a week*

2. He goes to the library every day. ____

3. He goes shopping once a week. ____

4. He takes guitar lessons on Wednesday mornings. ____

5. He plays tennis twice a week. ____

6. He does the laundry three times a week. ____

7. He sees his parents on the weekends. ____

8. He cleans the house on Saturday mornings. ____

**Grammar** **B Now answer these questions about Craig's schedule.**

1. How often does he go to the gym?   He goes to the gym twice a week.                    .
2. When does he have classes?   _____ .
3. How often does he go to a club?   _____ .
4. What does he do on Thursday nights?   _____ .
5. When does he go to the movies?   _____ .
6. What does he do on Saturday afternoons?   _____ .
7. Who does he play tennis with?   _____ .
8. Where does he go on Saturday nights?   _____ .

# 3 About you

**Grammar and vocabulary**

**Write questions for a friend. Then answer your friend's questions.**

1. **You** Where do you go after class ?
   *(go after class)*

   **Friend** I meet some friends and go to a restaurant for dinner. How about you?

   **You** I . . .                                                     .

2. **You** _____ ?
   *(do your English homework)*

   **Friend** Before dinner. I don't do homework after dinner. How about you?

   **You** _____ .

3. **You** _____ ?
   *(do in your free time at home)*

   **Friend** I rent a movie, or I just relax in front of the TV with a friend. How about you?

   **You** _____ .

4. **You** _____ ?
   *(go on the weekends)*

   **Friend** I go to a restaurant or club. How about you?

   **You** _____ .

5. **You** _____ ?
   *(go out with)*

   **Friend** Oh, friends from school. How about you?

   **You** _____ .

## 1 How often?

**Grammar**  **A** Write the frequency adverbs in order in the chart below.

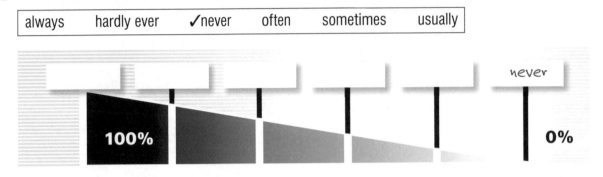

| always | hardly ever | ✓never | often | sometimes | usually |

never

100%    0%

**B** Answer the questions. Write true sentences using frequency adverbs.

**What's something you . . .**

1. hardly ever do before school / work?  _I hardly ever check my e-mail before school._

2. always do in the morning? _____

3. sometimes do after school / work? _____

4. never do during dinner? _____

5. often do in the evenings? _____

6. usually do on Saturdays? _____

## 2 What kinds of TV shows do you know?

**Vocabulary**  **A** Write the kinds of TV shows under the pictures.

1.  _soap opera_     2. _____     3. _____     4. _____

5. _____     6. _____     7. _____     8. _____

**B** Circle the kinds of TV shows from part A in the puzzle. Look in these directions (→↓).

| T | C | S | I | T | C | O | M | E | T | I | S |
|---|---|---|---|---|---|---|---|---|---|---|---|
| E | A | O | E | D | H | P | O | R | H | I | H |
| L | R | E | A | L | I | T | Y | S | H | O | W |
| K | T | A | L | K | S | H | O | W | U | P | O |
| S | O | A | P | O | P | E | R | A | E | E | U |
| D | O | C | U | M | E | N | T | A | R | Y | N |
| A | N | O | O | T | H | E | J | E | I | W | S |
| Y | T | E | A | I | U | W | D | O | C | T | V |
| Y | C | G | A | M | E | S | H | O | W | L | Y |

## 3 *About you*

**Answer the questions. Give two pieces of your own information in each answer.**

1. Do you ever watch soap operas?  <u>Yes, I always watch them in the afternoons.</u>
<u>I love Susan Lucci.</u>

2. What sitcom do you hardly ever watch? _____
_____

3. How often do you watch documentaries? _____
_____

4. What talk shows do you like? _____
_____

5. When do you usually watch the news? _____
_____

6. How often do you watch reality shows? _____
_____

# Do you go straight home?

## 1 Asking questions in two ways

*Conversation strategies*

**Complete the conversations with the questions in the box.**

| | |
|---|---|
| Do you like French? | I mean, do you belong to any clubs? |
| ✓ Do you do anything special? | I mean, do you know a nice place? |
| Do you play baseball? | I mean, do you go every day? |

1. **Lisa** What do you do after work?

   <u>Do you do anything special?</u>

   **Debbie** Well, I go to the gym.

   **Lisa** Really? How often do you go?

   _____

   **Debbie** No, not every day. I go Mondays, Wednesdays, and Thursdays.

2. **Howard** Do you know the restaurants around here?

   _____

   **Mary** Well, I often go to a little place on Main Street. What kind of food do you like?

   _____

   **Howard** Yes, I do. I love French food.

3. **Paul** What do you do after school?

   _____

   **Tom** Well, yeah. I'm in the Sports Club.

   **Paul** Really? What do you play?

   _____

   **Tom** Well, no. We watch baseball on TV!

   **Paul** Oh.

# 2 Questions, questions

**Conversation strategies**

**Write a second question for each question below. Then write true answers.**

1. What's your teacher like?
   I mean, is she nice?

   Yes, she's very nice. I like her a lot.

2. How often do you have English class?
   _____

   _____

3. How do you get to school / work?
   _____

   _____

4. What do you do for fun on the weekends?
   _____

   _____

5. Do you read a lot?
   _____

   _____

6. Do you ever go to clubs?
   _____

   _____

# 3 About you

**Conversation strategies**

**Add frequency adverbs to make these sentences true for you.
Then use *I mean*, and write more information.**

1. I ____never____ go to the gym. _I mean, I can't stand gyms._
2. I _____ get home early. _____
3. I _____ see my friends during the week. _____
4. I _____ go on the Internet in the evening. _____
5. I _____ eat breakfast at school / work. _____
6. I _____ get up early. _____
7. I _____ eat out on Saturdays. _____
8. I _____ watch reality shows on TV. _____
9. I _____ go shopping on the weekends. _____
10. I _____ study English after dinner. _____

# Internet addicts

## 1 Paula's problem

Reading **A** Read Paula's e-mail. How many hours does Paula spend at the computer?

☐ 3 hours ☐ 4 or 5 hours ☐ 7 or 8 hours

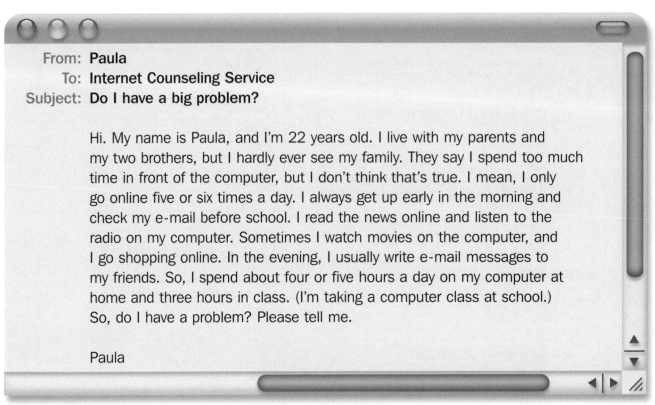

From: **Paula**
To: **Internet Counseling Service**
Subject: **Do I have a big problem?**

Hi. My name is Paula, and I'm 22 years old. I live with my parents and my two brothers, but I hardly ever see my family. They say I spend too much time in front of the computer, but I don't think that's true. I mean, I only go online five or six times a day. I always get up early in the morning and check my e-mail before school. I read the news online and listen to the radio on my computer. Sometimes I watch movies on the computer, and I go shopping online. In the evening, I usually write e-mail messages to my friends. So, I spend about four or five hours a day on my computer at home and three hours in class. (I'm taking a computer class at school.) So, do I have a problem? Please tell me.

Paula

**B** Read Paula's e-mail again. Then answer the questions.

1. Who does Paula live with? <u>She lives with her parents and her</u>
   <u>two brothers.</u>
2. Does she see her family a lot? _____
   _____
3. When does she check her e-mail? _____
   _____
4. Paula uses her home computer for six things. What are they? _____
   _____
5. What do you think? Does Paula have a problem? Why or why not?
   _____
   _____

# 2 I need some advice!

*Writing* **A** Read José's e-mail message. Complete it with *and* or *but*.

From: **José**
To: **Internet Counseling Service**
Subject: **Do I spend too much time at school?**

I think I have a problem. I don't have a computer at home, __but__ I use a computer at school. So, I usually go to school early, _____ I check my e-mail. I send e-mail to my friends in other countries. I often go online for fun, _____ sometimes I study English on the computer. Then on the weekends, I go to school _____ write papers for class (on the computer). Do I spend too much time at school?

**B** Write an e-mail message to the Internet Counseling Service about a problem you have. Write about a problem below, or use your own idea.

"I watch too much TV."      "I go shopping too much."      "I work too much."
"I stay home too much."      "I talk on my cell phone too much."      "I study too much."

From: _____
To: **Internet Counseling Service**
Subject: _____

_____
_____
_____
_____
_____
_____
_____

# Unit 5 Progress chart

| Mark the boxes below to rate your progress. ☑ = I know how to . . .   ? = I need to review how to . . . | To review, go back to these pages in the Student's Book. |
|---|---|
| **Grammar** | |
| ☐ ask simple present information questions | 44 and 45 |
| ☐ use time expressions like *once a week* | 44 and 45 |
| ☐ use frequency adverbs like *sometimes*, *never*, etc. | 46 |
| **Vocabulary** | |
| ☐ name at least 6 new free-time activities | 44 and 45 |
| ☐ name at least 6 kinds of TV shows | 47 |
| ☐ talk about likes and dislikes | 47 |
| **Conversation strategies** | |
| ☐ ask questions in 2 ways to be less direct | 48 |
| ☐ use *I mean* to repeat an idea and say more | 49 |
| **Writing** | |
| ☐ use *and* and *but* to link ideas | 51 |

## Nice places

### 1 What's in the neighborhood?

**Vocabulary** | Label the places in the picture. Use the words in the box.

| | | | | | |
|---|---|---|---|---|---|
| ✓apartment buildings | club | supermarket | restaurants | café | movie theater |
| fast-food places | park | museum | post office | stores | swimming pool |

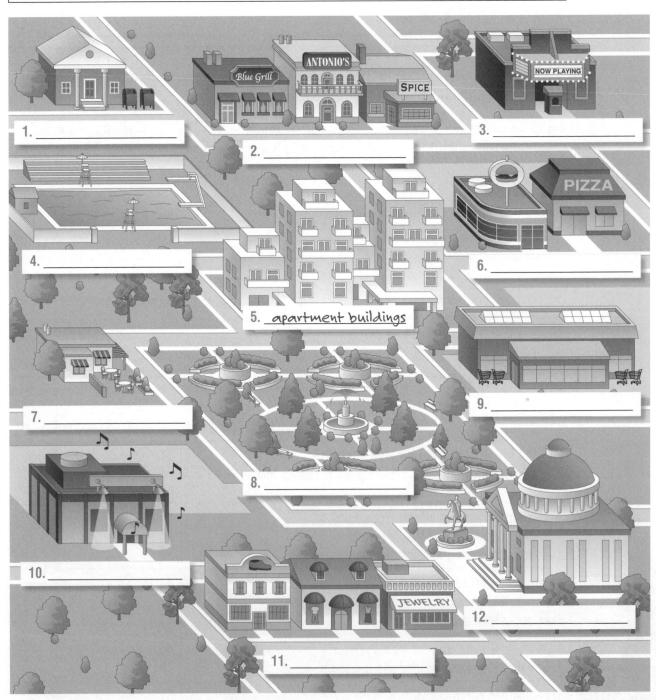

1. _____

2. _____

3. _____

4. _____

5. <u>apartment buildings</u>

6. _____

7. _____

8. _____

9. _____

10. _____

11. _____

12. _____

## 2 *Can you find the opposites?*

**Vocabulary**   Find six pairs of adjective opposites in the box. Write them in the chart below.

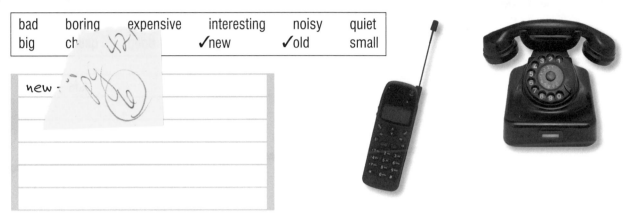

| bad | boring | expensive | interesting | noisy | quiet |
|-----|--------|-----------|-------------|-------|-------|
| big | ch~ |  | ✓new | ✓old | small |

new —

## 3 *That's not quite right!*

**Grammar**   Look at the picture on page 42. Correct the sentences to describe the neighborhood.

1. There's one cheap fast-food place.    *There are a couple of cheap fast-food places.*
2. There are a couple of post offices.    _____
3. There's a big stadium.    _____
4. There are a couple of supermarkets.    _____
5. There are some malls.    _____
6. There's an apartment building.    _____
7. There are no small stores.    _____
8. There's an expensive restaurant.    _____
9. There are a lot of beautiful parks.    _____
10. There's no movie theater.    _____

## 4 *About you*

**Grammar and vocabulary**   What's your neighborhood like? Complete the sentences with true information.

1. There's a _____ .
2. There are a lot of _____ .
3. There are some _____ .
4. There are a couple of _____ .
5. There's no _____ .
6. There are no _____ .

## 1 What's the time?

**A** Write the times in words. Where there are two lines, write the times two ways.

1. __It's three-thirty.__

2. _____

3. _____

_____

4. _____

_____

5. _____

_____

6. _____

_____

**B** Read about Kayo's day. Write the times in numbers. Then number the sentences in the correct order.

____ Her bus comes at __7:55__ (five to eight).

____ She gets home at _____ (nine-fifteen) and watches TV.

__1__ Kayo gets up at _____ (six-twenty-five).

____ She goes for lunch with her co-workers at _____ (noon).

____ She starts work at _____ (eight-forty-five).

____ She meets her boyfriend at _____ (twenty-five to six), and they have dinner.

____ She eats breakfast at _____ (twenty after seven).

____ She leaves work at _____ (ten after five).

____ She goes to bed at _____ (ten-thirty).

# 2 *Let's do it!*

**Grammar**  **Complete the conversations. Write questions starting with *What time*.
Use *Let's* to end each conversation with a suggestion.**

1.  *A*  I'm starving. Let's go to Burger Queen.

    *B*  But it's late. <u>What time does it close</u> ?

    *A*  It closes around 11:00, I think. _____ ?

    *B*  Almost 10:00. _____ .

2.  *A*  There's a new reality show on TV tonight.

    *B*  _____ ?

    *A*  Um, I think it starts at 8:00.

    *B*  Well, I'm really tired. _____ ?

    *A*  I'm not sure. I think it ends at 9:30.

    *B*  OK. _____ .

3.  *A*  Let's go to the gym on Saturday morning.

    *B*  Sure. _____ ?

    *A*  Oh, it opens early. At 6:00. _____ ?

    *B*  I usually get up around 8:00 on Saturdays.

    *A*  OK. _____ .

# 3 *About you*

**Grammar
and
vocabulary**  **Unscramble the questions. Then write true answers.**

1.  do / What time / get up / on weekdays / you ?

    *A*  <u>What time do you get up on weekdays?</u>

    *B*  _____

2.  your family / have / What time / does / lunch / on Sundays ?

    *A*  _____

    *B*  _____

3.  your English class / What time / start / does ?

    *A*  _____

    *B*  _____

4.  What time / leave home / do / you / in the morning ?

    *A*  _____

    *B*  _____

5.  stores / do / What time / in your neighborhood / open and close ?

    *A*  _____

    *B*  _____

# It's a great place to live.

## 1 Me too!

Circle the two correct responses to each comment. Cross out the incorrect response.

1. I think every neighborhood needs a park.
   a. ~~Me neither.~~
   b. (Me too)
   c. (Right)

2. We don't have a good fast-food place here.
   a. Yeah.
   b. Me too.
   c. I know.

3. I don't like the new restaurant.
   a. Yeah. I know.
   b. Me neither.
   c. Me too.

4. There are no good bookstores around here.
   a. I know.
   b. Me too.
   c. Right.

5. I like the new café downtown.
   a. Me neither.
   b. Me too.
   c. Right. It's good.

6. I love this neighborhood. It's so quiet.
   a. Right.
   b. Yeah, I know.
   c. Me neither.

## 2 What do they have in common?

Read the conversation. Are the sentences below true or false?
Then write *T* (true) or *F* (false).

*Glen* What's your new neighborhood like?

*Kirk* Oh, it's amazing. There are a lot of outdoor cafés and movie
theaters and clubs. I go out a lot.

*Glen* Really? I hardly ever go out in my neighborhood. It's boring.

*Kirk* Let's do something in my neighborhood this weekend.
I'm free on Saturday.

*Glen* Me too.

*Kirk* Well, there's a great jazz club near my apartment. I love jazz.

*Glen* Really? Me too!

*Kirk* But let's have dinner at a café first. The food at the club is
expensive, and I don't have a lot of money.

*Glen* Me neither. So, let's meet at 6:30 at your apartment.

1. Glen and Kirk both like their neighborhoods. __F__

2. Glen and Kirk both go out a lot in their neighborhoods. _____

3. Glen and Kirk are both free on Saturday. _____

4. Glen and Kirk both love jazz. _____

5. Glen and Kirk both have a lot of money. _____

> **Help note**
>
> *Glen and Kirk **both** love jazz.*
> *Glen loves jazz, **and** Kirk*
> *loves jazz, **too**.*

## 3 Right. I know.

Conversation
strategies

Circle the expression that is true about your neighborhood. Then show
you agree. Respond with *Right* or *I know*.

1. A (There are some)/ There are no good restaurants in our
   neighborhood.

   B ___I know._____

2. A Our neighborhood **has / doesn't have** a lot of great stores.

   B _____

3. A We live in a **great / terrible** neighborhood.

   B _____

4. A We **need / don't need** a shopping mall around here.

   B _____

## 4 About you

Conversation
strategies

Imagine you're talking to people from your neighborhood. Write true responses.

1. I really like this neighborhood.

   Me too. I think it's great.
   *or*
   Really? I don't like it very much.

2. I don't eat out in this neighborhood.
   _____

3. I think the restaurants are very expensive here.
   _____

4. I don't have a lot of friends around here.
   _____

5. I think our neighborhood is boring.
   _____

6. I think we need a couple of new stores in our neighborhood.
   _____

## 1 *Free events this weekend!*

**Reading** **A** Read the newspaper ads. Match the events with the pictures.
Write the correct numbers next to the pictures.

# Free Events This Weekend!

**1. All-City Pop Concert** Are you a fan of great singers and amazing bands? Come to the All-City Pop Concert. Meet local celebrities. Listen to exciting music. Dance!
The concert is Sunday at 8:00 p.m. in the cafeteria at Grant High School. There are only 200 seats, so come early.
Tickets are free.

**2. Parkview Food Festival** Do you love food? Do you often eat out? Then come to the Parkview Food Festival. Eat some delicious food from fifty different restaurants around the neighborhood — all for FREE!
*Saturday between 11:00 a.m. and 4:00 p.m. in Green Street Park.*

**3. Outdoor Street Fair** *Saturday and Sunday from 10:00 a.m. to 6:00 p.m. in front of the City Art Museum.*
There are a lot of beautiful items for sale — books, art, photos, paintings, CDs, and more.
Items for sale are just $2.00–$25.00.
Coffee, sodas, and snacks are for sale, too!

**4. Free Classes at the Neighborhood Center**
Do you want to take a class but don't have the money?
Try a free one-day class this Saturday. Learn:
- Art
- Spanish
- Music
- French
- Computers
- Yoga

Classes start at 10:00 a.m. and 2:00 p.m.
Go to www.freeclass.cup.org for more information.

**B** Read the ads again. Then answer the questions. Check (✓) the correct events.

| Which event(s) . . . | The pop concert | The food festival | The street fair | The free classes |
|---|---|---|---|---|
| 1. have food? | ☐ | ✓ | ✓ | ☐ |
| 2. are on Saturday? | ☐ | ☐ | ☐ | ☐ |
| 3. have a Web site? | ☐ | ☐ | ☐ | ☐ |
| 4. are during the day? | ☐ | ☐ | ☐ | ☐ |
| 5. are at night? | ☐ | ☐ | ☐ | ☐ |
| 6. are outdoors? | ☐ | ☐ | ☐ | ☐ |

# 2 Make your own event.

Writing **A** Complete the sentences with the prepositions in the box.

| at | at | at | between | for | ✓from | through | to |
|---|---|---|---|---|---|---|---|

1. The event is ___from___ 6:00 _____ 10:00.

2. The event is _____ 8:00 p.m. _____ the stadium.

3. Go to www.eventinfo.org _____ more information, or call Jim _____ 555-7777.

4. Call _____ 12:00 p.m. and 5:00 p.m., Monday _____ Friday.

**B** Imagine you are planning an event. Answer these questions. Use the ideas in the boxes and your own ideas.

| Events | | Places | |
|---|---|---|---|
| play | art exhibit | library | museum |
| concert | sporting event | park | theater |

1. What is the event? _____

2. When and where is it? _____

3. What time does it start and finish? _____

4. What's the cost of the event? Is it free? _____

5. What things are there to do at the event? _____

6. Where or how do people get more information? _____

**C** Now write an ad for your event from part B. Give the event a name.

_____
_____
_____
_____

# Unit 6 Progress chart

| Mark the boxes below to rate your progress.<br>✓ = I know how to . . .    ？ = I need to review how to . . . | To review, go back to these pages in the Student's Book. |
|---|---|
| **Grammar** | |
| ☐ use *There's* and *There are* with singular and plural nouns | 54 and 55 |
| ☐ use quantifiers: *a lot of*, *some*, *a couple of*, and *no* | 54 and 55 |
| ☐ use adjectives before nouns | 55 |
| ☐ ask and answer questions about time | 56 and 57 |
| ☐ make suggestions with *Let's* | 57 |
| **Vocabulary** | |
| ☐ name at least 6 adjectives to describe places | 54 and 55 |
| ☐ name at least 10 words for neighborhood places | 54 and 55 |
| ☐ give times for events | 56 and 57 |
| **Conversation strategies** | |
| ☐ answer *Me too* or *Me neither* to show I'm like someone | 58 and 59 |
| ☐ answer *Right* or *I know* to agree | 59 |
| **Writing** | |
| ☐ use prepositions *at*, *from*, and *to* with times and days | 61 |

# Unit 7 Out and about

**Away for the weekend**

## 1 What's the weather like?

**Vocabulary** | **A** Write two sentences about each picture.

1. It's hot.
   It's sunny.

2. _____
   _____

3. _____
   _____

4. _____
   _____

5. _____
   _____

6. _____
   _____

**B** Answer the questions. Write true answers.

1. How many seasons do you have in your city? What are they? _____
   _____

2. What's your favorite season? Why? _____
   _____

3. What kind of weather do you like? Cold weather? Hot weather? _____
   _____

4. What's the weather like today? Is it warm? _____
   _____

5. What's the weather usually like at this time of year? _____
   _____

6. Does it ever snow in your city? If yes, when? _____
   _____

## 2 I'm waiting for a friend.

**Complete the conversation. Use the present continuous.**

*Erin*  Hi, Ken. It's Erin. Where are you?

*Ken*  Oh, hi, Erin. I'm at the beach. I**'m spending**___ (spend) time with Tom. It's beautiful here today! It's, uh . . .

*Erin*  Nice. . . . I'm so happy you_____ (have) fun.

*Ken*  Yeah. We_____ (relax). We_____ (not do) anything special – I mean, I_____ (read) a book, and Tom _____ (swim). How about you? Are you at work?

*Erin*  No. I_____ (not work) today.

*Ken*  Oh, right. So, where – oops! Uh, I'm sorry. I_____ (eat) ice cream. I'm starving.

*Erin*  Yeah, me too. I_____ (eat) a cookie.

*Ken*  Really? So, where are you? I mean, are you at home?

*Erin*  No, I'm at Pierre's Café. I_____ (wait) for a friend. He's very late.

*Ken*  Oh, really? Who?

*Erin*  You!

## 3 About you

**Are these sentences true or false for you right now? Write *T* (true) or *F* (false). Then correct the false sentences.**

1.  _F_  I'm eating dinner right now.

    I'm not eating dinner right now. I'm doing my homework.

2.  _____  I'm using a computer.

    _____

3.  _____  My family is watching TV.

    _____

4.  _____  My friends are working.

    _____

5.  _____  It's snowing.

    _____

6.  _____  My best friend is skiing.

    _____

# Sports and exercise

## 1 All about sports

**A** Write the names of the sports or kinds of exercise under the pictures.

1. _____volleyball_____

2. _____

3. _____

4. _____

5. _____

6. _____

7. _____

8. _____

9. _____

**B** Complete the chart with the words in part A.

| People play . . . | People do . . . | People go . . . |
|---|---|---|
| volleyball | | |
| | | |
| | | |

**C** Answer the questions. Write true answers.

1. What sports do you play? How often?  _I play volleyball on Wednesday and_
   _basketball on the weekend._

2. What sports do your friends play? _____
   _____

3. Do you ever go biking? _____
   _____

4. What sports do people in your country like? _____
   _____

## 2 *What are you doing?*

Grammar : **Complete the conversations with present continuous questions.**

1. **Joe** Hey, Luis! _What are you doing_ (What / you / do) ?
   Are you at home?

   **Luis** No, I'm at the park. I'm playing tennis.

   **Joe** Really? _____ (you/ play)
   with Janet?

   **Luis** No, I'm playing with John today.

   **Joe** Oh. So, _____ (you / have / fun) ?

   **Luis** No, I'm not. You know, it's raining here, and it's cold.

   **Joe** That's too bad. _____ (you / play)
   right now? In the rain?

   **Luis** Yes, we are. And it's my turn to serve. Hold on a minute. . . .

   **Joe** So, um, _____ (you / win) ?

   **Luis** Uh, no. I'm not playing very well today.

   **Joe** Is it because you're talking on your
   cell phone?

2. **Janet** Hi, Kelly. _____ (How / you / do) ?

   **Kelly** Hi. Great. How are you? _____ (you / work)
   this summer?

   **Janet** Yes, I'm working at a gym. I'm teaching there. It's fun.

   **Kelly** Really? _____ (What / you / teach) ?

   **Janet** Aerobics.

   **Kelly** Cool. So, _____ (you / do) other things?
   I mean, _____ (you / swim), too?

   **Janet** Yeah. There's a pool at the gym. So, _____
   (you / do) anything special this summer?

   **Kelly** Well, no. I'm living in my sister's apartment. She's in
   San Francisco this summer.

   **Janet** Really? _____ (What / she / do)
   there?

   **Kelly** She's working in a restaurant.

   **Janet** _____ (she / meet) a lot of
   new people?

   **Kelly** Oh, yes. She's having a good time.

## 1 Keep the conversation going!

**Conversation strategies**   Complete the conversation with the follow-up questions in the box.

| | |
|---|---|
| Where are you working? | ✓ What are you doing? |
| Are you practicing your languages? | So, why are you studying Spanish and Portuguese? |
| What classes are you taking? | Are you enjoying your classes? |

*Alex* Hey, Kate. How's it going?

*Kate* Good. How are things with you?

*Alex* Great. But I'm really busy this summer.

*Kate* Really? <u>What are you doing?</u>

*Alex* Well, I'm taking a couple of classes, and I'm working.

*Kate* Wow! You're working and studying? _____

*Alex* I'm taking Spanish and Portuguese.

*Kate* That's interesting. _____

*Alex* Yeah, I really am. I'm learning a lot!

*Kate* That's great. _____

*Alex* Well, I'm thinking about a trip to South America.

*Kate* That's exciting!

*Alex* Yeah, and that's why I'm working two jobs, you know.

*Kate* Right. _____

*Alex* Well, I'm working at a Peruvian restaurant from 11:00 to 5:00, and I'm working at a Brazilian music club at night.

*Kate* Really? Wow! _____

*Alex* Yes, I am! I'm speaking Spanish all day and Portuguese all night.

*Kate* That's really cool! But when do you sleep?

*Alex* That's a problem. Sometimes I sleep in class.

*Kate* Oh, right. That *is* a problem.

## 2 *Asking follow-up questions*

Conversation strategies

**Complete two follow-up questions for each comment.**

1. "I don't play sports, but I often go running with a friend."

Really? Where _do you go running_ ?
How often _____ ?

2. "My parents are on vacation this month."

That's nice. Where _____ ?
Are they _____ ?

3. "My grandparents are visiting this week."

Really? Where _____ ?
How often _____ ?

4. "I'm working nights this summer."

Really? Where _____ ?
What time _____ ?

## 3 *Oh, that's good.*

Conversation strategies

**Read these people's comments about their summer activities. Complete the responses. Then ask a follow-up question.**

1. I'm really enjoying my vacation this summer.

Oh, that's _good_ .
_What are you doing_ ?

2. I'm not doing anything exciting. I'm just reading a lot.

That's _____ .
_____ ?

3. I'm not enjoying this summer at all. I'm working ten hours a day.

Really? That's _____ .
_____ ?

4. I'm just relaxing, and I'm watching a lot of TV.

Hey, that's _____ .
_____ ?

5. I'm exercising a lot at the gym this summer.

That's _____ .
_____ ?

6. What vacation? I'm painting my house right now.

Really? That's _____ .
_____ ?

## 1 An advice column

*Reading* **A** Which sports and exercises do you do? Check (✓) the boxes.

☐ aerobics ☐ biking ☐ skiing ☐ volleyball
☐ basketball ☐ running ☐ soccer ☐ weight training

**B** Read the advice column. Match the problems with the
Sports Professional's advice.

# Fitness talk

**Do you have a question about exercise? Write to Steven,
the Sports Professional, for help and good advice.**

**1. Amy**: I'm really busy this year. I'm going to school, and I'm working part-time at night. I like exercise, but I don't have a lot of time. Help! _____

**a. The Sports Professional:** Slowly add exercise to your weekly routine. Walk or ride a bike to work – don't drive. Use the stairs, not the elevator. Clean the house or do the laundry. Just do something – and start today!

**2. John:** I never exercise. I drive to work, and I sit all day. I hate sports, and I don't like the gym. I know it's a good idea to exercise, but how do I start? _____

**b. The Sports Professional:** You're right. You need a break. Try some different exercises. On Monday, do weight training. On Tuesday, go running. And on Wednesday, play basketball with friends. Each exercise helps your body in a different way. And it's always new and exciting!

**3. Bill:** I do weight training at the gym every day. I usually love exercise, but these days, it's boring. I think I need a break. What do you think? _____

**c. The Sports Professional:** Yes, I know the problem, but try and make time. Experts say we need 30 minutes of exercise 5 times a week. So do aerobics for 15 minutes in the morning. Go to school. Then go running for 15 minutes in the evening after work.

**C** Read the advice column again. Then answer the questions.

1. Amy is busy this year. What is she doing? _____
2. What is Amy's problem? _____
3. Is John getting enough exercise these days? _____
4. Does John like sports? _____
5. How often does Bill go to the gym? _____
6. What does Bill do at the gym? _____

# 2 Write your own advice.

Writing **A** Look again at the reading on page 56. Find five imperatives for advice.

*Try some different exercises.*

**B** Make imperatives for advice. Match the verbs with the words and expressions.

| (Don't) | be<br>buy<br>do<br>drive<br>exercise<br>watch | aerobics in the morning<br>at least five times a week<br>shy<br>some good running shoes<br>to work<br>TV all the time | *Don't be shy.*<br>*Buy some good running shoes.*<br><br><br><br> |

**C** Read the problems. Reply to each person. Give two pieces of advice using imperatives. Use the ideas above or your own ideas.

1. **Joe:** I watch sports on TV all the time. I'm watching the Olympics this month. It's great, but I don't do any sports. What sports are fun?
   **The Sports Professional:** *Try a lot of different sports. I like volleyball, tennis, and swimming. Also,*

2. **Anita:** This fall, we're playing soccer at school. I'm not enjoying it very much, especially when it's cold! Also, I'm not very good. Help!
   **The Sports Professional:**

3. **David:** I like exercise, but I'm lazy! I usually exercise for two or three weeks, but then I need a break. Do you have any advice?
   **The Sports Professional:**

## Unit 7 Progress chart

| Mark the boxes below to rate your progress.<br>☑ = I know how to . . .      ? = I need to review how to . . . | To review, go back to these pages in the Student's Book. |
|---|---|
| **Grammar** ☐ make present continuous statements<br>☐ ask present continuous questions | 66 and 67<br>68 and 69 |
| **Vocabulary** ☐ name at least 6 words to talk about the weather<br>☐ name at least 10 sports and kinds of exercise | 65, 66, and 67<br>67 and 68 |
| **Conversation strategies** ☐ ask follow-up questions to keep the conversation going<br>☐ react to things people say with *That's . . .* expressions | 70 and 71<br>71 |
| **Writing** ☐ use imperatives to give instructions and advice | 73 |

## 1 Do a crossword.

Vocabulary **A** Complete the crossword puzzle. Write the names of the clothes.

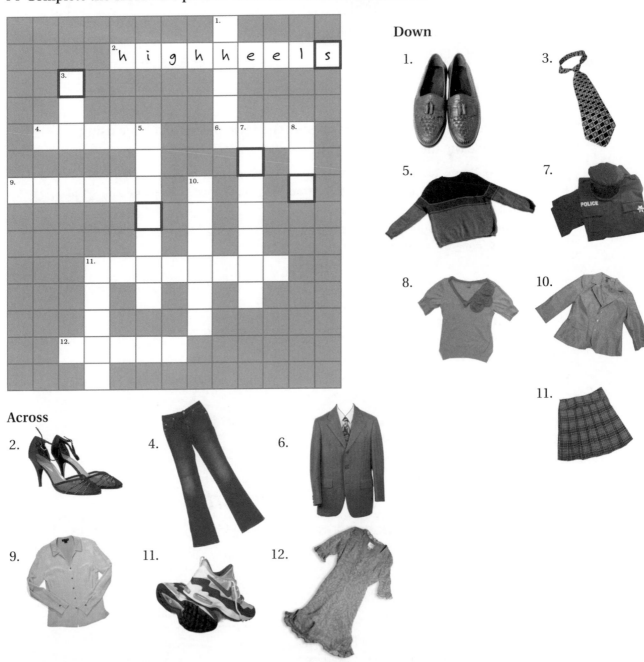

Down

1.
3.
5.
7.
8.
10.
11.

Across

2.
4.
6.
9.
11.
12.

**B** Now find the five highlighted letters in the puzzle. What do they spell?

\_\_\_\_ \_\_\_\_ \_\_\_\_ \_\_\_\_ _s_

## 2 I want to spend some money!

**Grammar**  Complete the conversations with the correct form of the verbs.

1. *Mia*  Let's go shopping. I ___need to buy___ (need / buy)
      some new clothes.

   *Rick*  OK. Where do you _____ (want / go) ?

   *Mia*  To the mall. I _____ (need / get)
      some new jeans. And I _____ (have / get)
      a couple of new suits for work.

   *Rick*  Listen. You go. I think I _____ (want / stay)
      home. I _____ (not need / buy) anything,
      and I _____ (want / check) my e-mail.

   *Mia*  OK!

2. *Will*  I have a date with Megan tonight. She _____ (want / go)
      to an expensive restaurant.

   *Ana*  Really? Do you have any good clothes?
      Those old jeans are terrible. And you know Megan –
      she _____ (like / wear) designer clothes.

   *Will*  I know, but I _____ (like / wear) my jeans!
      And I _____ (not want / go) to a
      restaurant anyway. I _____ (want / go)
      to a movie.

   *Ana*  Oh, there's the phone. Hello? . . . Will, it's Megan.
      She's sick.

   *Will*  Oh, no! Well, now I _____ (not have / change)
      my clothes!

## 3 About you

**Grammar and vocabulary**  Unscramble the questions. Then write true answers.

1. *A* to the movies / do / like / What / to / wear / you ? ___What do you like to wear to the movies?___
   *B* _____

2. *A* nice / have / When / do / to / clothes / you / wear ? _____
   *B* _____

3. *A* you / Do / a / have / uniform / to / wear ? _____
   *B* _____

4. *A* new / buy / you / jeans / need / Do / to ? _____
   *B* _____

5. *A* clothes / do / What / want / you / buy / to ? _____
   *B* _____

6. *A* do / go / like / Where / you / to / shopping ? _____
   *B* _____

# Things to buy

## 1 Accessories

Write the words under the pictures.

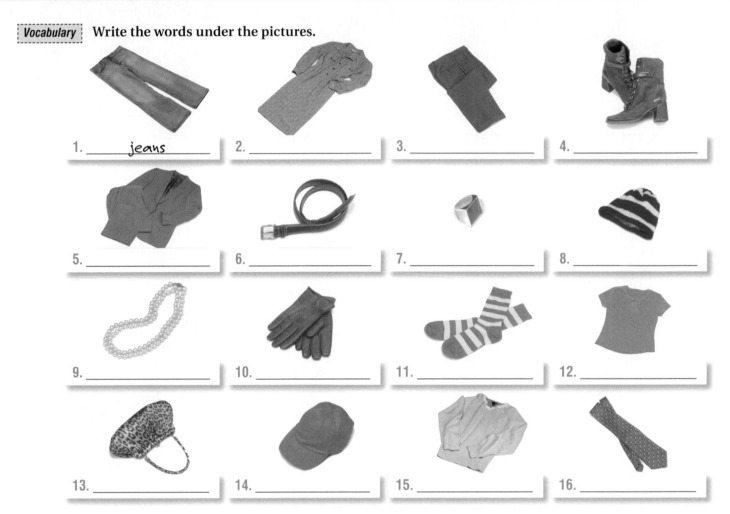

1. ___jeans___
2. _____
3. _____
4. _____

5. _____
6. _____
7. _____
8. _____

9. _____
10. _____
11. _____
12. _____

13. _____
14. _____
15. _____
16. _____

## 2 Colors

Complete the color words in the box. Then answer the questions, and complete the chart.
Write three colors to answer each question, if possible.

| r e d     y_____w     b_____k     p_____e     w_____ |
| o_____e     b___e     g_____n     b_____n     g___y |

| What colors . . . | | | |
|---|---|---|---|
| do you like to wear? | blue | | |
| are you wearing right now? | | | |
| do you never wear? | | | |
| are in your home? | | | |
| are your favorites? | | | |
| are popular right now? | | | |
| are in your country's flag? | | | |

60

## *3 How much is this?*

**Grammar** | **A** Complete the conversations. Use *this*, *that*, *these*, or *those*.

1. *Lena* Um, excuse me. How much is ___that___ dress?
   *Clerk* The red dress? It's $325.
   *Lena* Oh. And how about _____ shoes?
   *Clerk* They're $149.
   *Lena* Oh, really. And what about _____ T-shirts? Are they expensive, too?
   *Clerk* They're $49.
   *Lena* Oh, well. Thanks anyway.

2. *Ting* Excuse me.
   *Seller* Yes?
   *Ting* How much are _____ umbrellas?
   *Seller* They're $19.99.
   *Ting* $19.99? Really?
   *Seller* Oh, wait. Sorry. _____ umbrella is $4.99. _____ umbrellas over here are $19.99.
   *Ting* OK, so I want _____ umbrella, please.

**B** Look at the pictures. Write questions and answers.

1.

**$18.00**

A ___How much are those scarves___?
B _____.

2.

**$99.99**

A _____?
B _____.

3.

**$40.00**

A _____?
B _____.

4.

**$325.99**

A _____?
B _____.

**Can I help you?**

## 1 Um, uh, oh!

Complete the chart with the "conversation sounds" and expressions in the box.

| Really? | ✓I know. | Let's see. | Oh. | Yeah. | Well |
|---|---|---|---|---|---|
| Uh-huh. | Right. | Let me think. | Uh | Um | |

| You want to show you agree. | You are surprised. | You need time to think. |
|---|---|---|
| I know. | | |
| | | |
| | | |
| | | |

## 2 About you

Answer the questions with true information. Start each answer with a "time to think" expression.

1. What's your favorite color?
   Let me think . . . I guess it's green. _____

2. What's your favorite thing to wear? _____

3. How often do you go shopping for clothes? _____

4. How much do jeans cost these days? _____

5. How many birthday presents do you have to buy this month? _____

6. Does your family like to shop for clothes together? _____

# *3 Are you listening?*

**Complete the conversation with the correct expressions.**

*Roberto*  Mom, I have to get some things for college.

*Mother*  _____Uh-huh._____ What do you need to get?
          (Uh-huh. / Let me think.)

*Roberto*  _____ . . . I need to get a new computer and . . .
           (Um, let's see. / Really!)

*Mother*  _____ They're expensive.
          (Let me think. / Oh, really?)

*Roberto*  I know. But I have to go online a lot for my classes.

*Mother*  Well, OK. And what else do you want?

*Roberto*  _____ I want to get a cell phone and . . .
           (Uh-huh. / Uh, well . . .)

*Mother*  _____ that's a good idea. I'm surprised. I mean,
          (Oh, / Um,)

          you usually don't call, so . . .

*Roberto*  Right. So I need to get a cell phone. _____ Oh, yes, and
                                                 (Let's see. / Uh-huh.)

           I have to get an alarm clock.

*Mother*  _____ You need an alarm clock. You always get up late.
          (Let me think. / Uh-huh.)

*Roberto*  And what else? _____ What else do I need to get?
                          (Oh, really? / Uh, let's see.)

*Mother*  Well, there's one more thing you need to get . . .

*Roberto*  What's that?

*Mother*  A job for some money for these things!

# Shop till you drop!

## 1 Online shopping

Reading **A** Read the article. Who likes to shop online? Who doesn't like to shop online? Check (✓) the correct boxes.

|  | *Likes to shop online* | *Doesn't like to shop online* |
|---|---|---|
| *Sarah* | ☐ | ☐ |
| *Matt* | ☐ | ☐ |
| *Kevin* | ☐ | ☐ |
| *Susana* | ☐ | ☐ |

## Do you like to shop online?

These days, everything is for sale online – cars, computers, movie tickets, and even houses. But why is online shopping so popular? Fans say it's easy. But not everyone likes to shop on the Internet. What do you think of it?

**Sarah Cho**

"I never shop on the Internet because you need to have a credit card. You know, I don't have a credit card, and I don't want a credit card. And I don't like to spend a lot of time online."

**Matt Carson**

"I work long hours – from 8:00 in the morning to 7:00 or 8:00 at night. A lot of stores close at 8:00. But the Internet never closes. I mean, I often shop at 1:00 in the morning. And the prices online are usually really cheap."

**Kevin Parker**

"There isn't a shopping center near my house. I have to drive an hour to the mall. Online shopping is very convenient. I buy DVDs, books, clothes, and even food online. I never need to go out to a store."

**Susana Rivera**

"I like to shop with friends. We get up early and go the mall together. We have a great time. We have lunch and look at the clothes together. When you shop online, you don't spend time with friends. You're alone."

**B** Read the article again. Then write *Sarah*, *Matt*, *Kevin*, or *Susana* next to the statements.

1. "I don't like to shop online because I like to pay cash." _____Sarah_____
2. "I like to shop online because I never have to leave my home." _____
3. "I like to shop online because the prices aren't expensive." _____
4. "I don't like to shop online because I like to go to the mall with friends." _____
5. "I like to shop online because the hours are convenient." _____
6. "I don't like to shop online because I don't like to go on the Internet." _____

# 2 *What do you think?*

Writing **A** Why do people like to shop online? Why do people hate to shop online?
Check (✓) the correct box.

| I like to shop online . . . | I hate to shop online . . . | Reasons |
|---|---|---|
| ☐ | ✓ | because I always buy things I don't need |
| ☐ | ☐ | because it's easy to compare prices |
| ☐ | ☐ | because it's convenient |
| ☐ | ☐ | because you don't always have to pay sales tax |
| ☐ | ☐ | because I often get "spam" e-mails from shopping Web sites |

**B** Answer these questions. Try to write more than *Yes* or *No.*

1. Do you live near a mall or shopping center? _____

2. Do you have time to shop during the week? _____

3. Do you like to go online? _____

4. Do you use credit cards? _____

**C** Write a short paragraph. Use your ideas from part B, and give reasons. Start like this:
*I like to shop online because . . .* **or** *I don't like to shop online because . . . .*

_____
_____
_____
_____
_____

## Unit 8 Progress chart

| Mark the boxes below to rate your progress. ✓ = I know how to . . .   ? = I need to review how to . . . | To review, go back to these pages in the Student's Book. |
|---|---|
| **Grammar** ☐ use *like to, want to, need to,* and *have to* with other verbs | 76 and 77 |
| ☐ ask questions with *How much . . . ?* | 78 and 79 |
| ☐ use *this, these, that,* and *those* | 79 |
| **Vocabulary** ☐ name at least 12 kinds of clothes | 75, 76, and 77 |
| ☐ name at least 12 personal items | 78 and 79 |
| ☐ name at least 8 color words | 78 |
| **Conversation strategies** ☐ use expressions like *Um . . .* and *Let's see . . .* | 80 |
| ☐ use *Uh-huh* and *Oh* to show that I agree or I'm surprised | 81 |
| **Writing** ☐ use *because* to give reasons | 83 |

# Unit 9 A wide world

**Sightseeing**

## 1 Take a tour!

**Vocabulary**  **A** Complete these suggestions for tourists.

1. In South Korea, visit
   ___an island___ .

2. In New York, take pictures
   from a _____ .

3. In Germany, visit an old
   _____ .

4. See a _____
   of a famous writer in Paris.

5. In Rio de Janeiro, spend a day
   at the _____ .

6. In Egypt, walk around the
   _____ .

7. In London, see a famous
   _____ .

8. Go up a _____ and
   get a good view in Tokyo.

9. Take a _____ of
   the city in Sydney.

**Grammar and vocabulary**  **B** Can you do any of the things in part A in your city or town? Write four true sentences.

1. _In my area, you can visit an island._ **or** _In my area, you can't visit an island._

2. _____

3. _____

4. _____

5. _____

## 2 *What can you do in Toronto?*

**A** Read the guidebook. What can you do in Toronto? Complete the chart below.

# Toronto, Canada

## Things to do . . .

### 1. The CN Tower
Get a good view of the city from 553 meters (1,814 feet).
A restaurant, shops, and a glass floor!
*Hours: 10:00 a.m. to 11:00 p.m.*

### 2. Casa Loma
Toronto's only castle. Call for a tour.
*Open 9:30 a.m. to 5:00 p.m.*
*(Last entry at 4:00 p.m.)*

### 3. Yorkville
Walk around a lively historic neighborhood!
Outdoor cafés, shops, and movie theaters.

### 4. The Art Gallery of Ontario
*Hours: 10:00 a.m. to 6:00 p.m.*

### 5. Centre Island
Take the ferry to Centre Island.
Enjoy beautiful parks, great
restaurants, and a children's
amusement park.
*Open all day.*

### 6. Ontario Place
Everything you want!
During the day: a water park, boats for rent, movies, and many
children's areas. In the evening: restaurants, a club, movies, or
see an outdoor concert.
*Park open 10:00 a.m. to 8:00 p.m.*
*Outdoor concerts start at 8:00 p.m.*

| On a rainy day | On a sunny day | In the evening | With children |
|---|---|---|---|
| You can go to the Art Gallery of Ontario. | | | |
| | | | |

**B** Complete the conversations with *can* or *can't*.

1.  **Jill** What __can__ you do at Ontario Place?

    **Dan** Let's see . . . you _____ go to a water park and rent a
    boat. And at night, you _____ go to an outdoor concert.

    **Jill** Sounds great! _____ we go right now?

    **Dan** No, we _____ . It opens at 10:00, and it's only 7:30 now.
    It's really early.

    **Jill** Oh, you're right. Well, _____ we go to a café for breakfast?

    **Dan** Yes, we _____ do that. Let's go!

2.  **Yoshi** I'm tired today. I don't want to go on another walking
    tour! Where _____ we go to relax?

    **Keiko** Let's go to Yorkville. We _____ have a nice lunch and
    see a movie.

    **Yoshi** OK, but we _____ spend a lot of money. We need to
    save our money for shopping!

## 1 What countries do you know?

**Vocabulary**

**A** Complete the names of the countries. Then write the countries in the chart below.

1. S _p_ ai _n_
2. ___ ___ str ___ l ___ ___
3. ___ or ___ cc ___
4. C ___ st ___ ___ ic ___
5. R ___ ss ___ ___

6. M ___ x ___ c ___
7. P ___ r ___
8. Fr ___ nc ___
9. S ___ ___ th K ___ r ___ ___
10. Ch ___ n ___

11. Th ___ ___ l ___ nd
12. I ___ d ___ ___
13. J ___ p ___ n
14. C ___ n ___ d ___
15. Br ___ z ___ l

| | | | |
|---|---|---|---|
| *I know a lot about . . .* | | | |
| *I don't know a lot about . . .* | | | |
| *They speak English in . . .* | | | |
| *I love the food from . . .* | | | |
| *I don't want to go to . . .* | | | |

**B** Look at the pictures. What kinds of food are these dishes? Write the nationalities.

1. _Japanese_ _____    2. _____

3. _____    4. _____

**C** Complete the chart.

| Food I like | Food I don't like | Food I want to try | Food I can cook |
|---|---|---|---|
| Korean | | | French |
| | | | |
| | | | |
| | | | |
| | | | |

## 2 *Where in the world?*

**Vocabulary** Complete the crossword puzzle.

| | | | | | | | | | |
|---|---|---|---|---|---|---|---|---|---|
| 1. | | | | | | | | | |
| 2. A | N | 3. T | A | R | C | T | 4. I | C | 5. A |
| | | | | | | | | | |
| | | 6. | | | | | | | |
| | | | | | | | | | |
| 7. | | | | | 8. | | | | |
| | | | | | | | | | |
| | 9. | | | | | | | | |
| | | | | | 10. | | | | |
| | | | | | | | | | |

**Across**

2. There are no cities in this cold, icy region.
6. This country is in both Europe and Asia.
7. This large region includes Japan and South Korea.
9. Beijing, Shanghai, and Hong Kong are in this country.
10. This long, thin country is in South America.

**Down**

1. They speak both French and English in this North American country.
3. They speak this language in Turkey.
4. Rome, Venice, and Milan are cities in this European country.
5. This large country is in Oceania.
8. They speak this language in Thailand.

## 3 *About you*

**Grammar** Unscramble the questions. Then write true answers.

1. can / sports / play / What / your best friend ?

   A  What sports can your best friend play?

   B _____

2. food / mother / make / Can / Mexican / your ?

   A _____

   B _____

3. speak / you / languages / can / What ?

   A _____

   B _____

4. your / speak / English / parents / Can ?

   A _____

   B _____

# They're a kind of candy.

## 1 What's this? What are these?

What are the things in the pictures? Write sentences. Use the words in the box.

| candy | drink | sandwich | ✓musical instrument | shoe | sport |

1. It's a kind of musical instrument. It's called an **erhu**.

2. They're a kind of ___ They're called ___

3. ___

4. ___

5. ___

6. ___

70

## 2 *What's an* Inukshuk?

**Complete the sentences. Then unscramble the letters from the boxes to find the answer to the question.**

1. A sneaker is a kind of  s h o e .
2. A *tortilla* is kind of like a  p __ __ __ a __ __ .
3. A *bouzouki* is like a  g __ __ t __ __ .
4. A *hanbok* is a kind of traditional  o □ t __ __ t .
5. *Lassi* is kind of like a  __ __ k s __ __ e .
6. Volleyball is a kind of  __ p __ r □ .

What's an *Inukshuk*?

It's like a  s __ __ t __ e .

## 3 *It's a kind of pot.*

**Complete the conversations. Use *like*, *kind of like*, or *a kind of*.**

1. *A* That's a beautiful dish!
   *B* Thanks. Actually, it's _a kind of_ pot. It's Japanese.
   *A* Can you cook with it? It looks so pretty.
   *B* Yeah! You can make Japanese food _____ *yosenabe* in it.
   *A* Like what?
   *B* Yosenabe. It's _____ soup.

2. *A* What can you buy at the market?
   *B* Well, you can buy food from different countries, things _____ fruit. You can buy durians . . .
   *A* What's a durian?
   *B* It's _____ fruit.
   *A* Really?
   *B* Yeah. It's _____ a melon.
   *A* Is it good?
   *B* Yes, I love it.

# Exciting destinations

## 1 FAQs about Paris

**Reading** **A** Read the Web page. Write the correct question heading for each paragraph.

Where can you eat in Paris?    ✓What are great places to visit in Paris?
What do people wear in Paris?    How can I travel around Paris?

# The PARIS Page

*The Paris Page* is a Web site about Paris. The information is from people like you. Please <u>send a message</u> and share information about your trip to Paris!

## Frequently Asked Questions (FAQs)

### <u>What are great places to visit in Paris?</u>

You have to see the <u>Eiffel Tower</u> on your first visit. Then go to the <u>Louvre</u>. It's a very large and famous art museum. There are also beautiful gardens near it. After that, you can visit the <u>Latin Quarter</u>. It's a very old neighborhood. It has a lot of historic buildings, museums, and great shopping. <u>More</u> . . .

It's easy to travel in Paris. There are trains, buses, and subways. Try the subway system, called the <u>Metro</u>. There are 368 Metro stations in the city. Every building in Paris is near a Metro station, so it's very convenient, too! <u>More</u> . . .

Parisians love food. There are amazing <u>cafés</u>, <u>bistros</u>, and other kinds of <u>restaurants</u> everywhere in the city. You can relax at an outdoor café all day. Cafés open early in the morning and usually close at about 10:00 p.m. <u>More</u> . . .

Parisians like to "dress up" and wear <u>designer clothes</u>. They never wear shorts, sneakers, or T-shirts to restaurants or concerts. You can wear casual clothes and shoes in Paris, but try to look nice. <u>More</u> . . .

<u>Next</u>

**B** Read the Web page again. Then write *T* (true) or *F* (false) for each sentence. Correct the false sentences.

1. The Louvre is a famous garden in Paris.  _F_  _The Louvre is a famous art museum in Paris._

2. The Latin Quarter is a historic building. ___ _____

3. The Metro is a museum in Paris. ___ _____

4. A bistro is a kind of restaurant. ___ _____

5. Cafés open late in Paris. ___ _____

6. Parisians like to wear casual clothes when they go out. ___ _____

## 2 *FAQs about your country*

*Writing* **A** Complete each sentence with three things about your city or country.
**Make lists and use commas.**

1. <u>Salvador</u> is famous for <u>its beautiful beaches, outdoor markets, and great food</u> .

2. _____ is famous for _____ .

3. There are great places to see. You can visit _____ .

4. The people usually wear _____ .

**B** Imagine you are looking at a travel Web site about your country or city.
**Write answers to these questions.**

**TRAVEL**

1. I often travel there on business, but I don't usually have a lot of time. Where can I go and what can I see in one day?

   _____

   _____

   _____

2. I want to visit this summer, but I don't have a lot of money. What can I do for free?

   _____

   _____

   _____

3. Where can I meet local people? What traditional things can I see or do?

   _____

   _____

   _____

## *Unit 9 Progress chart*

| **Mark the boxes below to rate your progress.**<br>☑ = I know how to . . .  ? = I need to review how to . . . | To review, go back to these pages in the Student's Book. |
|---|---|
| **Grammar**   ☐ use *can* and *can't* to talk about things to do in a city | 86 and 87 |
| ☐ use *can* and *can't* to talk about ability | 88 and 89 |
| **Vocabulary**   ☐ use at least 10 new sightseeing words | 86 and 87 |
| ☐ name at least 15 countries and 5 regions | 88 |
| ☐ name at least 10 nationalities and 10 languages | 88 and 89 |
| **Conversation strategies**   ☐ use *a kind of* and *kind of like* to explain new words | 90 |
| ☐ use *like* to give examples | 91 |
| **Writing**   ☐ use commas to separate items in a list | 93 |

## A night at home

### **1** *What did they do last night?*

**Grammar**  What did these people do last night? What didn't they do? Complete two sentences for each picture. Use the simple past.

**stay home / visit her parents**

1. Kate __stayed home__ .

   She __didn't visit her parents__ .

**watch TV / practice her guitar**

2. Rita _____ .

   She _____ .

**study English / cook dinner**

3. Mee Sun _____ .

   She _____ .

play chess / watch a DVD

4. Ali and Sam _____ .

   They _____ .

**listen to CDs / e-mail friends**

5. Emil _____ .

   He _____ .

**invite friends over / clean the house**

6. Joe and Ken _____ .

   They _____ .

## 2 *How was your weekend?*

Grammar | Complete Grace's e-mail. Use the simple past.

---
e-mail

To: Paulina Lopez
From: Grace Chen
Subject: How was your weekend?

Hi Paulina!

I really ____enjoyed____ (enjoy) the weekend! I _____ (invite)
a friend over on Saturday. She's my co-worker, and she's very nice.
We _____ (play) tennis in the morning and _____
(stay) at the tennis club for lunch. Then we _____ (practice)
yoga and _____ (walk) in the park.

In the evening, we _____ (watch) a DVD and _____
(cook) a big dinner. We _____ (talk) a lot, but we
_____ (not talk) about work. And we _____
(not watch) TV all day – a nice change!

Then on Sunday, I _____ (study) English and _____
(clean) the house. Hey! You _____ (not call) me on Sunday!
Call me soon, OK? Tell me about your weekend.

Grace

---

## 3 *About you*

Grammar
and
vocabulary | Write true sentences about your weekend. Use the simple past.

1. invite a friend over    <u>I invited a friend over.</u>      <u>I didn't invite a friend over.</u>

2. stay home    _____

3. study for an exam    _____

4. clean the house    _____

5. call a friend    _____

6. check my e-mail    _____

7. chat online    _____

8. practice my English    _____

9. listen to music    _____

10. rent a DVD    _____

11. cook a big meal    _____

12. exercise    _____

# A busy week

## 1 A weekly planner

Read Jenna's planner. Then complete the sentences below. Use the simple past of
the verbs in the box.

| Sunday | Monday | Tuesday | Wednesday |
|---|---|---|---|
| Movie with Meg 1:00 ✔ <br><br> Romeo and Juliet – Ford Theater 2:00 ✗ <br><br> Homework ✗ | Read The Pearl. ✔ <br><br> Read art magazine. ✗ <br><br> Homework ✔ | Write book report on The Pearl. ✔ <br><br> Write history paper. ✗ <br><br> Homework ✔ | Piano lesson 4:30 ✗ <br><br> Doctor's appointment 2:00 ✔ <br><br> Homework ✔ |

| Thursday | Friday | Saturday | |
|---|---|---|---|
| Call: Mom ✔ <br>     Felipe ✔ <br>     Lia ✔ <br><br> Make dinner 6:30. ✗ <br><br> Homework ✔ | Alison's party 7:30 ✔ <br><br> Mike 8:00 ✗ <br><br> Homework ✔ | Shopping! Need new: <br>     shoes ✗ <br>     jacket ✔ <br><br> Homework ✗ | |

| buy | do | go | have | make | read ✔ | see | write |
|---|---|---|---|---|---|---|---|

1. On Sunday, Jenna __saw__ a movie.
   She __didn't see__ a play.

2. On Monday, Jenna _____ a book in English.
   She _____ a magazine.

3. Jenna _____ a book report on Tuesday.
   She _____ a history paper.

4. Jenna _____ a doctor's appointment on Wednesday.
   She _____ a piano lesson this week.

5. On Thursday, Jenna _____ a lot of phone calls.
   She _____ dinner.

6. On Friday, Jenna _____ to a party.
   She _____ out with Mike.

7. Jenna _____ a new jacket on Saturday.
   She _____ new shoes.

8. Jenna _____ homework every school day.
   She _____ homework on the weekend.

## 2 About you

Grammar and vocabulary

**A** Complete the questions in the questionnaire. Use the simple past of the verbs in the box. Then write true answers. Write more than *yes* or *no*.

| do | ✓go | see | eat | take | have | make | speak | write |

# Questionnaire: *Did you . . . ?*

**1.** _Did_ you _go_ out a lot last week?
Yes, I did. I went out every night last week. **or** No, I didn't. I stayed home.

**2.** _____ you and your family _____ dinner in front of the TV last night?
_____

**3.** _____ you _____ anything interesting last weekend?
_____

**4.** _____ you _____ in a restaurant on Friday night?
_____

**5.** _____ your class _____ a test or an exam last week?
_____

**6.** _____ you _____ dinner every night last week?
_____

**7.** _____ your best friend _____ you an e-mail yesterday?
_____

**8.** _____ your parents _____ a movie on Saturday night?
_____

**9.** _____ you _____ to a lot of friends at school yesterday?
_____

**B** Write a sentence about each day last week. Write one thing you did each day.

1. (Monday) _____
2. (Tuesday) _____
3. (Wednesday) _____
4. (Thursday) _____
5. (Friday) _____
6. (Saturday) _____
7. (Sunday) _____

**I'm exhausted!**

## 1 Responding to news

**Conversation strategies**

**A** Complete the conversations. Choose and write the best response.

1. *A* I bought a new TV today.

   *B* _Good for you!_

   a.)Good for you!
   b. You poor thing!
   c. Good luck!

2. *A* I'm 25 today!

   *B* _____

   a. You poor thing!
   b. Good luck!
   c. Happy birthday!

3. *A* My wife had a baby girl last night.

   *B* _____

   a. Good for you!
   b. Happy birthday!
   c. Congratulations!

4. *A* I started a great new job last week.

   *B* _____

   a. You poor thing!
   b. Good for you!
   c. Happy birthday!

5. *A* My English exam is this afternoon.

   *B* _____

   a. Good for you!
   b. Congratulations!
   c. Good luck!

6. *A* I worked late every day last week.

   *B* _____

   a. You poor thing!
   b. Thank goodness!
   c. Good for you!

**B** Your "friend" tells you some news, and you respond. Write the conversations.

1. Your friend bought a new car, and he got a bargain.

   I bought a new car today. I got a bargain.

   Good for you!

2. Your friend got 100% on her English exam.

3. Your friend finally got a job.

4. Your friend wanted to go on vacation, but he has no money.

# 2 *You did?*

**A** Complete the conversations with the expressions in the box.

| ✓You did? | You did? | You did? | Good luck! | That's too bad. | Good for you. |
|---|---|---|---|---|---|

1. *Lilly* Did you have a busy day?

   *Beth* Yeah, I'm exhausted. I went shopping downtown.

   *Lilly* _____You_____ _____did?_____ Did you buy anything?

   *Beth* Yes, I bought a new suit. And a blouse and shoes.

   *Lilly* _____ _____ _____

   *Beth* And then I had lunch with Maria, and we talked all afternoon. How about you?

   *Lilly* I cleaned the house, did the laundry, and made dinner.

   *Beth* _____ _____ That's great! I'm starving! Let's eat!

2. *Jun* Did you have a good week?

   *José* Actually, no. I had five exams.

   *Jun* _____ _____ That's awful. Did you pass?

   *José* Well, I passed three and failed two.

   *Jun* Oh. _____ _____ _____

   *José* And I have two exams tomorrow, too.

   *Jun* _____ _____ Study hard!

**B** Write two responses for each piece of news.

1. I had a terrible vacation in Hawaii.

   _____You did?_____ _____You poor thing!_____

2. I took my driver's test yesterday.

   _____ _____

3. I wrote an article for a magazine last month.

   _____ _____

4. Pierre and I worked all weekend.

   _____ _____

## 1 A busy birthday . . .

**Reading** **A** Look at the four pictures. Then read Peter's blog (online journal). Number the pictures in order from 1 to 4.

---

**FRIDAY, MAY 28**                    **11:45 p.m.**

I had a crazy day today. I had an English exam, and it's my birthday!

I had the exam at 8:30 this morning. I needed to study, so I woke up early – at 6:30 a.m. I took a shower, made some coffee, and studied for about an hour. Well, the coffee didn't work. I fell asleep! I woke up at 8:20 with my head on my books. I had ten minutes before the test started!

I ran outside, got on my bike, and went to English class. I got there right at 8:30, but guess what! The teacher never came! My classmates and I waited about half an hour. Then we left. It's great. Now I can really study for the exam.

I had breakfast, and then I went to my next class – math. ☹ I think math is really hard, but I have to take it. My teacher talked for an hour. I wanted to write some notes, but I fell asleep. I need to borrow my friend's notes.

After I finished class, I met my friend Louisa, and we went to a movie together. It was my birthday, so she paid! Great! We saw the new Nicole Kidman movie. You know, I usually like her movies a lot, but I didn't like this movie very much.

When I got home from the movie, my mother called and sang "Happy Birthday" to me. Now I think I have to stay up and finish a paper for a class tomorrow. I hope I don't fall asleep again!

**Posted by Peter Miller @ 11:45 p.m.**

0 comments

---

**B** Read the blog again. Then answer the questions. Give reasons for the *no* answers.

1. Did Peter get up late? __No, he didn't. He needed to study._____

2. Did Peter take an English exam? _____

3. Did he listen to his math teacher? _____

4. Did he go out with a friend? _____

5. Did Peter's mother call? _____

6. Do you think he's a good student? _____

## 2 *My last birthday*

Writing **A** Read the blog on page 80 again. Match the two parts of each sentence.

1. Peter studied when __c__
2. Peter had breakfast after ____
3. When Peter went to his math class, ____
4. Peter finished classes. Then ____
5. Peter saw a movie before ____

a. he went home.
b. he fell asleep again.
c. he got up in the morning.
d. he met his friend Louisa.
e. he left his English class.

**B** Now think about a day you remember well. Answer these questions. Write more than *yes* or *no.*

1. Did you work or have classes? _____

2. Did you go out with friends? _____

3. Did you do something fun? _____

_____

4. Did you eat any of your favorite foods? _____

_____

5. Did you go to any stores? _____

_____

6. Did you get home late? _____

**C** Now write a paragraph for your own blog. Use your ideas from part B.
Use *before, after, when,* or *then,* if possible.

I remember my last birthday. I _____

_____

_____

## Unit 10 Progress chart

| Mark the boxes below to rate your progress. ☑ = I know how to . . .    ? = I need to review how to . . . | To review, go back to these pages in the Student's Book. |
|---|---|
| **Grammar**  □ make simple past statements with regular verbs  □ make simple past statements with irregular verbs  □ ask simple past *yes-no* questions | 98 and 99  100 and 101  101 |
| **Vocabulary**  □ make simple past forms of at least 12 regular verbs  □ make simple past forms of at least 8 irregular verbs  □ use time expressions with simple past | 98 and 99  100 and 101  101 |
| **Conversation strategies**  □ use responses like *Good for you!* and *Congratulations!*  □ use *You did?* to show I'm listening, surprised, or interested | 102 and 103  103 |
| **Writing**  □ use *before, after, when,* and *then* to order events | 105 |

## Lesson A My first . . .

### 1 Yesterday

**Vocabulary** Complete the sentences. Use the words in the box.

| busy | ✓happy | nervous | nice | quiet | scared |

1. Yesterday was my birthday. My friends had a party for me, and I got a lot of presents. I was very __happy__ .
2. My family and I live in a very small town. There are no clubs or movie theaters. My town is really _____ – especially at night.
3. I started a new job yesterday. I was really _____ of my new boss.
4. I had a lot of things to do yesterday. I was pretty _____ .
5. My best friend's parents are friendly. They're very _____ .
6. We had a French test last week. I was really _____ , but I passed.

### 2 It was fun!

**Vocabulary** Choose the best two words to complete each sentence. Cross out the wrong word.

I remember my first driving lesson. Before I met the teacher, I was really ~~scary~~ / **nervous** / **scared**. But then I relaxed because he was very **nice** / ~~strict~~ / **friendly**. The lesson was ~~awful~~ / **good** / **fun** because I didn't make a lot of mistakes. I was pretty good. At the end of the lesson, I was **exhausted** / ~~lazy~~ / **tired**. It was hard work! After ten lessons I took my test, but I didn't pass. I wasn't ~~awful~~ / **pleased** / **happy**. But I passed three weeks later. Now I can drive my dad's **nice** / **new** / ~~awful~~ car.

# *3 I remember . . .*

**Grammar** **Complete the conversations with *was, wasn't, were,* or *weren't*.**

1. *Sally* Do you remember your first date, Grandpa?

   *Grandpa* Yes. I __was__ 16, and the girl _____ in my class.

   We _____ classmates. We went to the movies.

   *Sally* _____ you nervous?

   *Grandpa* No, I _____ . It _____ a lot of fun.

   *Sally* Do you remember her name?

   *Grandpa* Yes. Grandma!

2. *Paula* I remember my first day in high school.

   It _____ a hot day, and I went with

   two of my friends.

   *Kenton* _____ you scared?

   *Paula* No, we _____ really scared, but I

   guess we _____ a little nervous.

   *Kenton* _____ the teachers friendly?

   *Paula* Yes, they _____ very nice.

   Thank goodness.

3. *Sun Hee* Do you remember your first college English class?

   *Carla* Yes, it _____ last year. I _____ very good at

   English, and I made a lot of mistakes. My partner's

   English _____ very good, so he _____

   very happy with me!

   *Sun Hee* _____ he smart? I mean, intelligent?

   *Carla* Yes, he _____ .

   *Sun Hee* So, was your first class fun?

   *Carla* No, it _____ . In fact,

   it _____ awful.

# Vacations

## 1 About you

**A** Unscramble the questions. Then write true answers.

1. trip or vacation / was / last / your / When ?

   *A* <u>When was your last trip or vacation?</u>

   *B* _____

2. go / did / Where / exactly / you ?

   *A* _____

   *B* _____

3. weather / like / was / the / What ?

   *A* _____

   *B* _____

4. you / there / do / did / What ?

   *A* _____

   *B* _____

5. were / there / How / you / long ?

   *A* _____

   *B* _____

**B** Read about Emi's first trip to the park with a friend. Write questions for the answers.

"We weren't very old – I think I was eight and my friend was ten. We went to the park, but my mother didn't know. We had a great time! We went swimming in the pool. I remember it was a beautiful day – warm and sunny. We were there about an hour. Then we got hungry, so we went home. When we got back, my mother wasn't too happy."

1. *A* <u>How old was Emi?</u>

   *B* Eight.

2. *A* _____

   *B* To the park.

3. *A* _____

   *B* Her friend.

4. *A* _____

   *B* They went swimming.

5. *A* _____

   *B* Warm and sunny.

6. *A* _____

   *B* About an hour.

## 2 Get *and* go

**A** Which of these expressions do you use with *get*? Which do you use with *go*? Which can you use with *get* and *go*? Complete the chart.

| | | | | | |
|---|---|---|---|---|---|
| ✓back | to bed | scared | swimming | to the movies | a view of something |
| lost | a gift | skiing | (an) autograph | snorkeling | along with someone |
| ✓home | hiking | camping | on vacation | a bad sunburn | to see a concert/movie |
| sick | biking | married | up early or late | on a road trip | |

| *get* | *go* | *get* and *go* |
|---|---|---|
| back | | home |
| | | |
| | | |
| | | |
| | | |
| | | |
| | | |
| | | |
| | | |
| | | |

**B** Complete the questions with *get* or *go*. Then write your own answers.

1. *A* What time do you _____go_____ to bed on weeknights?

   *B* _____

2. *A* How often do you _____ swimming?

   *B* _____

3. *A* Did you _____ a bad sunburn last year?

   *B* _____

4. *A* What did you _____ for your last birthday?

   *B* _____

5. *A* Can you think of someone you don't _____ along with?

   *B* _____

6. *A* Where do you want to _____ on vacation this year?

   *B* _____

7. *A* Do you ever _____ to see bands?

   *B* _____

**How was your weekend?**

## 1 Asking questions

Conversation
strategies

**Complete each conversation with two questions.**

1. *Sadie*  How was your weekend?

   *Bill*  It was awful. We went hang gliding. I hated it!

   *Sadie*  That's too bad.

   *Bill*  Yeah. Anyway, how about you?

   <u>What did you do?</u>

   <u>Did you do anything interesting?</u>

   *Sadie*  Well, we rented a car and went camping.

   *Bill*  That sounds nice.

2. *Dirk*  Did you go out last night?

   *Leo*  Yeah, I met a friend and went to a club.

   _____

   _____

   *Dirk*  Oh, I went to the Laundromat and did the
   laundry. I didn't do anything exciting.

3. *Shira*  I went to the concert last Saturday.

   *Jaz*  I did, too! The band sounded great.

   _____

   _____

   *Shira*  Oh, it was fantastic. Well, anyway, it's 11:30.

   *Jaz*  Yeah, it's late. See you tomorrow.

4. *Gabor*  So, did you work last weekend?

   *Koji*  Yeah, Saturday and Sunday. We were really busy.

   _____

   _____

   *Gabor*  Let's see . . . I went shopping, um, and saw
   a movie. Then on Sunday, I played tennis,
   made dinner . . .

   *Koji*  I guess you were busy, too!

# 2 *Well, anyway . . .*

**A** Use *Anyway* three times in this conversation. Leave two of the blanks empty.

*Mirka* Where were you last week? Were you away?

*Arlen* Yes, I was in Mexico on business.

*Mirka* Mexico? What was that like?

*Arlen* Oh, great. The customers there are really nice. _____ I always enjoy my trips to Mexico. The people are so friendly.

*Mirka* That's nice. _____ So you're traveling a lot these days.

*Arlen* Yeah. About six times a year. _____ , what about you? Did you have a good week?

*Mirka* Not bad. I had a lot of meetings – you know, the usual. _____ , do you want to go out tonight? We can have dinner maybe.

*Arlen* Sure. We can meet after work.

*Mirka* OK. Well, _____ , I have to go. See you later.

**B** Use the instructions to complete the conversations.

1. *Friend* What do you usually do on the weekends?

    *You* <u>I usually go out with friends. What about you?</u>
    (*Answer. Then ask a question about your friend.*)

    *Friend* Me? I usually go to see a movie. Sometimes a friend and I go camping or hiking.

2. *Friend* I'm enjoying my new job. My boss is OK, and the people are nice. We get along – it's a friendly place.

    *You* That's nice. _____
    (*Change the topic. Invite your friend for dinner.*)

    *Friend* Tomorrow? Sounds great. What time? Seven?

3. *Friend* What did you do for your last birthday?

    *You* _____
    (*Answer. Then end the conversation. It's late.*)

    *Friend* OK. Talk to you later.

4. *Friend* So how was your weekend?

    *You* _____
    (*Answer. Then change the topic. Talk about next weekend. Invite your friend.*)

    *Friend* Sure. Sounds like fun.

*A funny thing happened . . .*

## 1 My first job

**A** Read the story. What are these people like? Match the names with the adjectives.

1. Diana __*a*__
2. Joe _____
3. Megan _____
4. Rick _____

a. friendly
b. nervous
c. good-looking
d. strict

# Tell Us About Your First Job

*Reader Megan Walker writes in with a story about her first job.*

I remember my first job. I worked in an outdoor café one summer. It was called Sunny's. I got free drinks and food. My boss Diana was very friendly, and I got along well with her. Her husband Joe worked there, too, but he was really strict. On my first day, I was late because I got lost on the subway. After that, Joe was never too happy with me.

So, every day I served sandwiches and coffee. But the café was really busy all the time. I wasn't a very good server, so I was usually nervous. And I was always exhausted by the end of the day.

One day, I was really tired, so I asked to go home early. Joe looked angry, but he said, "OK. Fine." I left and went to the subway. But then I met my friend Rick on the street. He was really good-looking, and I liked him a lot. He said, "Do you want to go and eat something?" I said, "Yes. OK. Where?" And he said, "I know a café near here. Let's go there. They have good sandwiches."

So we went back to Sunny's and sat down to eat! We waited for about ten minutes before Joe finally came over to the table. He was very busy, so he didn't look at me. He said, "I'm sorry. One of the servers left early. Are you ready to order?" We stayed for an hour. I was lucky – my boss never saw me. But I had to pay for my sandwich and soda!

– *Megan Walker*
*New York City*

**B** Read Megan's story again. Then answer the questions.

1. Where did Megan work? _She worked at Sunny's._____

2. How did Megan get to work? _____

3. What kind of food did she serve? _____

4. What was the café like? _____

5. Why did she leave early one day? _____

6. Why did she go back to Sunny's? _____

7. How long did they stay at Sunny's? _____

# 2 He said, . . .

**A** Read the rest of the story. Rewrite their conversation after they leave the café. Use quoted speech. Add capital letters and correct punctuation (" " , . ?).

Rick and I left the café and talked for a few minutes.

rick asked how did you like the café    <u>Rick asked, "How did you like the café?"</u>

I said it's nice   _____

he said the service wasn't very good   _____

I said well one of the servers left early   _____

rick said people are so lazy these days   _____

I said yes I know   _____

But I didn't tell Rick I was the server!

**B** Think about a different story – the time you met your first best friend. Answer these questions.

1. How old were you? _____

2. What was your best friend's name? _____

3. How did you first meet? What happened? _____

4. What did you say when you first met? I said, "_____."

5. What did your best friend say? She said, "_____."

**C** Now write a story about your best friend. Use your ideas from part B.

My first best friend's name was _____ . _____

_____

_____

_____

_____

## Unit 11 Progress chart

| Mark the boxes below to rate your progress.<br>☑ = I know how to . . .    ? = I need to review how to . . . | To review, go back to these pages in the Student's Book. |
|---|---|
| **Grammar**<br>☐ make simple past statements and questions with *be*<br>☐ ask simple past information questions | 108 and 109<br>110 |
| **Vocabulary**<br>☐ name at least 12 words to describe people or experiences<br>☐ name at least 4 new expressions with *go*<br>☐ name at least 5 new expressions with *get* | 108 and 109<br>111<br>111 |
| **Conversation strategies**<br>☐ ask and answer questions to show interest<br>☐ use *Anyway* to change the topic or end a conversation | 112<br>113 |
| **Writing**<br>☐ use captials and punctuation in quoted speech | 115 |

## 1 Mmmmm!

**Vocabulary** Write the names of the foods. Then find the words in the puzzle. Look in these directions (→↓).

1. ___meat___

2. ___seafood___

3. _____

4. _____

5. _____

6. _____

7. _____

8. _____

| F | F | V | C | A | R | R | O | T | S |
|---|---|---|---|---|---|---|---|---|---|
| R | X | E | B | I | B | E | E | F | S |
| U | O | G | A | X | R | M | E | A | T |
| I | A | E | N | S | E | I | S | T | A |
| T | E | T | A | E | A | L | L | C | E |
| G | G | A | N | A | D | K | F | H | P |
| P | G | B | A | F | R | U | I | E | P |
| O | S | L | S | O | P | P | D | E | A |
| T | F | E | N | O | U | D | L | S | S |
| A | I | S | Z | D | I | H | G | E | T |
| T | S | H | R | I | C | E | F | Q | A |
| O | H | C | H | I | C | K | E | N | M |
| E | C | U | C | U | M | B | E | R | S |
| S | H | E | L | L | F | I | S | H | Z |

9. _____

10. _____

11. _____

12. _____

13. _____

14. _____

15. _____

16. _____

17. _____

18. _____

## 2 An invitation to dinner

**Grammar**  **A** Circle the correct words to complete the e-mails.

Invitation to *a dinner party*
On *Saturday night*
At *7:30 p.m.*
At *my house*
Bring friends! *Jenny*

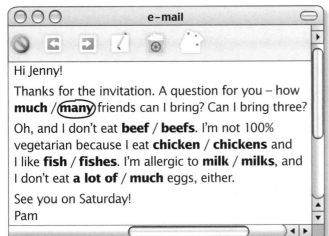

e-mail

Hi Jenny!

Thanks for the invitation. A question for you – how **much** / **many** friends can I bring? Can I bring three?

Oh, and I don't eat **beef** / **beefs**. I'm not 100% vegetarian because I eat **chicken** / **chickens** and I like **fish** / **fishes**. I'm allergic to **milk** / **milks**, and I don't eat **a lot of** / **much** eggs, either.

See you on Saturday!
Pam

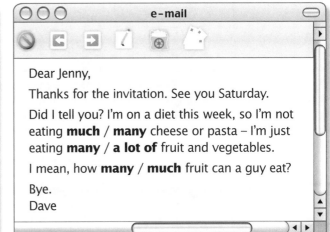

e-mail

Dear Jenny,

Thanks for the invitation. See you Saturday.

Did I tell you? I'm on a diet this week, so I'm not eating **much** / **many** cheese or pasta – I'm just eating **many** / **a lot of** fruit and vegetables.

I mean, how **many** / **much** fruit can a guy eat?

Bye.
Dave

**B** Write your own e-mail to Jenny. Include the topics below.

- the food you like
- the food you don't like
- food you eat a lot of
- food you don't eat a lot of

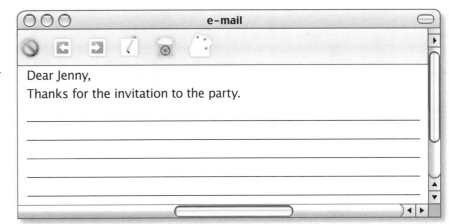

e-mail

Dear Jenny,
Thanks for the invitation to the party.

_____

_____

_____

_____

## 3 About you

**Grammar and vocabulary**

Complete the questions with *How much* or *How many*. Then write your own answers.

1. _How many_ students in your class are vegetarians? _____

2. _____ milk does your family buy every week? _____

3. _____ times a week do you eat chicken? _____

4. _____ shellfish do you eat? Do you eat a lot? _____

5. _____ of your friends are picky eaters? _____

6. _____ cans of soda do you drink a day? _____

# What's for dinner?

## 1 At the supermarket

| Vocabulary | Write the words under the pictures. Then write the food in the chart below.

1. apples

2.

3.

4.

5.

6.

7.

8.

9.

10.

11.

12.

13.

14.

15.

16.

17.

18.

19.

20.

| meat and seafood | fruit | vegetables | other |
|---|---|---|---|
| | apples | | |
| | | | |
| | | | |
| | | | |
| | | | |
| | | | |

## 2 *What would you like?*

**Grammar** — **Complete the conversations. Use *would you like* or *'d like*.**

1. *Jim* What __would you like__ ?
   *Megan* I_____ ice cream, please.
   *Jim* _____ chocolate sprinkles?
   *Megan* Yes, please.

2. *Server* Good evening. _____ something to drink?
   *Dan* Oh, just water, please.
   *Server* OK. And what _____ to eat?
   *Dan* Um, I_____ the salmon, please.
   *Server* _____ some green beans with it?
   *Dan* Actually, I_____ some spinach, please.

3. *Greg* Where _____ to go for dinner?
   *Sheila* Oh, I don't know. I_____ to go somewhere around here.
   *Greg* _____ to try the new Thai restaurant?
   *Sheila* Oh, yes! I_____ something spicy.

## 3 Some *or* any

**Grammar** — **Complete the conversations with *some* or *any*.**

1. *Ming* Polly, try __some__ lamb.
   *Polly* Gosh, it's hot! I need _____ water . . . now!
   *Ming* Here. Drink _____ soda.

2. *John* Do you have _____ chocolate cookies?
   *Ken* No, but we have _____ peanut butter cookies.
   *John* OK, I'll take _____ .

3. *Sara* Would you like _____ potato chips?
   *Craig* Yeah, but I can't buy _____ . I don't have _____ money.

**Let's take a break for lunch.**

## 1 A sandwich or something

Complete the conversation with *or something* or *or anything*.

**Trish** Do you go out for lunch every day or . . . ?

**Pete** Well, I don't usually eat lunch. I don't like to eat a big meal _or anything_ at lunchtime.

**Trish** No? You don't have a snack _____ ?

**Pete** Well, I sometimes have a hot drink, like hot chocolate _____ .

**Trish** Well, I'm hungry – I'd like a sandwich _____ . Would you like something to eat?

**Pete** Well, maybe . . .

**Trish** How about a salad _____ ?

**Pete** Yes, OK. Actually, I'd like a chicken sandwich. Oh, and let's get some ice cream _____ , too. I guess I *am* hungry!

## 2 About you

Answer the questions. Write true answers. Use *or something* or *or anything*.

1. Are you a picky eater?  Well, I don't eat fish or shrimp or anything.

2. What do you usually have for dinner? _____

3. How about lunch? _____

4. What do you like to order in restaurants? _____

5. What do you drink with meals? _____

6. What kinds of snacks do you like? _____

# *3* *Would you like to go out or . . . ?*

Conversation
strategies **Which questions can end with *or . . . ?* Add *or . . .* where possible.**

1. *Paul* What would you like for dinner tonight _____ ?

    Would you like to go out _or . . ._ ?

   *Val* Yes, please! I'd love to eat out.

   *Paul* That's great. So can I choose the restaurant _____ ?

   *Val* Sure.

   *Paul* Let's see . . . would you like a pizza _____ ?

   *Val* Um, I don't want Italian tonight. How about an
    Asian place? Do you like Korean or Thai _____ ?

   *Paul* Uh, I don't really care for spicy food.

   *Val* Let me think . . . do you want to get a hamburger _____ ?

   *Paul* Yeah! With maybe some French fries,
    and some cookies.

   *Val* OK! Stop! I'm starving! Let's go!

2. *Kate* It's my birthday today.

   *Sally* Happy birthday! Do you have plans _____ ?

   *Kate* I had plans, but my friend just called. He's sick.

   *Sally* That's terrible! I know. Let's eat at my house. I can
    cook some steaks or something. What do you
    think _____ ?

   *Kate* That's very nice, thanks, but I'm a vegetarian.

   *Sally* Oh. Do you eat pasta _____ ?

   *Kate* Well, I can't eat pasta or anything heavy right
    now. I'm on a diet.

   *Sally* OK. No pasta. What would you like _____ ?

   *Kate* Do you have any fruit _____ ?

   *Sally* Sorry. I ate the last banana this morning
    before I went to work. I have some carrots. . . .

   *Kate* Let's stop at the supermarket on our way
    to your house.

# Great places to eat

## 1 The first "theme" restaurant

**Reading** **A** Read the article. Find the answers to these questions.

1. Where did the first Hard Rock Cafe open? _____
2. How many Hard Rock Cafes are there now? _____
3. How many rock 'n' roll souvenirs do they have? _____

Two Americans opened the first Hard Rock Cafe in London in 1971. They started the restaurant because they didn't like the hamburgers in England. They thought people would like American-style food, and they were right. The restaurant became very popular because it had good prices, friendly service, and a casual atmosphere.

Now, there are about 110 Hard Rock Cafes in 41 countries – from Hollywood to Kuala Lumpur. They all have the usual American foods (hamburgers, French fries, and milk shakes), loud rock 'n' roll music, and lots of teenage customers.

The first Hard Rock Cafe had a fun, American atmosphere, but it didn't always have a rock 'n' roll theme. Then one day, a famous musician named Eric Clapton gave the restaurant his guitar. They put the guitar on the wall. Then one week later, Pete Townshend – a musician for the band The Who – gave his guitar to the restaurant. So they put that on the wall, too.

Now, Hard Rock Cafes around the world have about 60,000 rock 'n' roll souvenirs. These souvenirs include guitars and other kinds of instruments, posters, costumes, and photos. And they always get new things.

After over 30 years, the restaurant is still popular with both tourists and famous celebrities. There are always crowds outside Hard Rock Cafes. People like to visit the different restaurants and buy T-shirts with the names of the different cities. And both famous rock stars and local musicians sometimes visit and give free concerts for the customers. The Hard Rock is still rockin'!

**B** Read the article again. Then correct these sentences.

1. The first Hard Rock Cafe opened in ~~Hollywood.~~ *London*
2. The Hard Rock Cafe serves British food.
3. The restaurant atmosphere is very formal.
4. There are Hard Rock Cafes in 110 countries.
5. Pete Townshend gave the restaurant its first guitar.
6. The Hard Rock Cafe in London has 60,000 souvenirs.
7. These days, the restaurant isn't crowded.
8. Many musicians visit the restaurants and buy T-shirts.

# 2 Restaurant reviews

**A** Jill Heacock is a restaurant reviewer. She ate at the Seafood Palace last week, and she loved it. Circle the correct words to complete Jill's review.

---

## This week's restaurant: The Seafood Palace ★ ★ ★ ★

**by Jill Heacock**

Last week, I went to the Seafood Palace – it's a **terrible** / **wonderful** restaurant. I loved it. I was there on a busy night, and the atmosphere was **fun** / **formal**. The food was **awful** / **delicious**, and every dish came to the table **cold** / **hot**. I really liked the shrimp. Very tasty! The service was **excellent** / **slow**, the servers were really **friendly** / **lazy**, and the meal was **cheap** / **expensive**. I only spent $12! The Seafood Palace is a good place to hang out with friends or have dinner with your family. Try it!

---

**B** Imagine you are a restaurant reviewer. You ate at a restaurant, and you hated it. Write your review.

---

## This week's restaurant: _____ ★

**by** _____

Last week, I went to _____ – it's a terrible restaurant! _____

_____

_____

_____

_____

_____

---

# Unit 12 Progress chart

| Mark the boxes below to rate your progress.  ☑ = I know how to . . .    ? = I need to review how to . . . | To review, go back to these pages in the Student's Book. |
|---|---|
| **Grammar** |  |
| ☐ use countable and uncountable nouns | 118 and 119 |
| ☐ make statements and questions with *much, many,* and *a lot of* | 118 and 119 |
| ☐ make statements and questions with *some, any,* and *not any* | 120 and 121 |
| ☐ make offers and requests with *would like* | 121 |
| **Vocabulary** |  |
| ☐ name at least 5 categories of food | 118 and 119 |
| ☐ name at least 25 different foods | 118, 119, and 120 |
| **Conversation strategies** |  |
| ☐ use *or something* and *or anything* | 122 |
| ☐ use *or . . . ?* in *yes-no* questions to make them less direct | 123 |
| **Writing** |  |
| ☐ use expressions to talk about restaurants | 124 and 125 |

## Illustration credits

## Photography credits

## Text credits

**Notes**

*Notes*